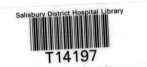

WHJ 1207

A Colour Atlas of
INJURY IN SPORT
Second edition

J.G.P. Williams
MD, MSc, FRCS, FRCP

Consultant in Rehabilitation Medicine, Wexham Park Hospital, Slough
Civil Consultant in Rehabilitation Medicine, Royal Navy
(formerly Medical Director, Farnham Park Rehabilitation Centre
Secretary General, International Federation of Sports Medicine
Honorary Secretary, British Association of Sport and Medicine)

Wolfe Medical Publications Ltd

Copyright © J.G.P. Williams, 1990
Second edition published by Wolfe Medical Publications Ltd, 1990
Printed by Smeets-Weert, Holland
ISBN 0 7234 1531 5

First edition published by Wolfe Medical Publications Ltd, 1980

A CIP catalogue record for this book is available from the British Library.

This book is one of the titles in the series of Wolfe Medical Atlases, a series that brings together the world's largest systematic published collection of diagnostic colour photographs.

For a full list of Wolfe Medical Atlases, plus forthcoming titles and details of our surgical, dental and veterinary Atlases, please write to Wolfe Publishing Ltd, 2-16 Torrington Place, London WC1E 7LT.

Contents

Preface

It has been very exciting to note how the practice of sports medicine and the management of injuries in sport have attracted more and more attention in the years since this Atlas was first published. Greater understanding of the underlying causes and factors in the development of injury in sport and the steady evolution and expansion of the techniques of diagnosis and treatment are reflected in the increase in the size and scope of this new edition.

It has been possible to incorporate much of the useful and constructive ideas and criticism received since the Atlas first appeared. New and better illustrations of a number of conditions and injuries have become available, refinements in imaging techniques – particularly CT and MR scanning – have clarified diagnosis, while the number of off-beat and unusual presentations continues to intrigue and astonish. Many well-known conditions, such as a fractured clavicle, can now be depicted in a variety of different presenting forms, and it has also been possible to illustrate several new rarities for which clinical material has become available.

As with the first edition, the basic material included here forms the basis of lectures on injuries in sport presented in the United Kingdom and abroad. The same principle of focusing attention primarily on those injuries which are peculiar to sport, and seldom encountered outside the sporting context, prevails. However, as before, injuries of a wider incidence are also included where they have particular relevance to sport (for example, severe ligament injuries of the knee).

There has been some improvement in the general pattern and layout of the Atlas, and a number of additional diagrams have been provided – for example, those showing common sites of tendon injury and stress fracture in sport. Where appropriate, legends accompanying illustrations have been developed to provide greater explanation; in the case of the mechanical aspects of injury, in direct response to the interest shown in the Atlas by lay sportsmen and women.

I am delighted to have had the opportunity to update and enlarge the Atlas, which I hope will continue to demonstrate the extraordinarily wide range of clinical problems associated with sport – many of which form an increasingly important part of everyday general, accident and orthopaedic practice.

Acknowledgements

I would like to thank my friends and colleagues:

Barbara Ansell, David Bell, Sue Boardman, John Buck, Graeme Campbell, Sheila Christian, John Davies, Patrick England, Ennis Giordani, David Hirschowitz, Jack Kanski, Philip Kerr, Chris Lewis, James Moncur, Robert Nagle, Nigel Tubbs and Leon Walkden for additional material; Andrew Dent for helping to put it all together; The Editors of *Sports Medicine, Medisport, British Journal of Sports Medicine, Journal of Bone and Joint Surgery* and *Medicine* for permission to use material previously published; Derek Griffin, Clinical Photographer at Wexham Park Hospital, for his help with the clinical photographs; and Don Morley and Tony Duffy of All Sport for their magnificent portfolio of colour action photographs which have given real life to the Atlas.

In preparing the second edition I would like to add my particular thanks to Michael Edgar, John King and James Robertson for their useful suggestions for modifications and especially to John Buck who has provided a wealth of useful tips and ideas which I have incorporated in this new edition. I am particularly grateful to Peter Dovey and Roderick Grant for their help, specifically with radiological and other imaging material. I am also grateful to Jean Tyler, Clinical Photographer at Wexham Park Hospital, and Daphne Bannister, Clinical Photographer at King Edward VII Hospital, both of whom have helped with the provision of new material.

For Sally,
Stephen, Philippa and David,
again with love

1 Nature and incidence of injury in sport

The term 'sports injury' is something of a misnomer. Injury is the result of the application to the whole body or part of the body of forces which exceed the ability to adjust to them. These forces may be applied instantaneously or over a considerable period. The exact nature of the injury – the tissues involved and the way in which the damage is sustained – depends upon the mechanism by which excess force is applied. The body is able to differentiate between different types of stress (for example, the tissue response to a direct blow is different from that to a sudden stretch), but it is not able to differentiate between the different activities in which one particular mechanical type of violence is applied.

Most injuries sustained in sport are essentially no different from those sustained in other activities. However, the degree of damage, particularly secondary damage such as haemorrhage and haematoma formation, may be greater in the sportsman because (a) training affects tissue states and (b) exercising tissue is metabolically more active than tissue at rest. In addition, the demand of the patient in terms of rehabilitation and return to activity may be significantly greater.

From a practical point of view studies of patients attending clinics for sports injuries show that a very substantial majority of problems could be well handled either by general practitioners, hospital accident and emergency departments (in America, 'emergency rooms'), or by hospital specialists in appropriate disciplines as part of their normal practice. However, there are numerous injuries and clinical problems which are peculiar to sport (though the number unrelated to ordinary day-to-day activities is relatively small), and sporting injuries do require particular expertise in their diagnosis and management.

The extent and severity of the injury are modified by a number of factors including the general physical and psychological fitness of the patient, his or her constitutional suitability for the sport, environmental conditions at the time of the injury, age and sex and general level of nutrition. The victim's general level of skill and proficiency is also significant. It is interesting to note how in body-contact sport most severe injuries occur in the first quarter of the game, whereas the last quarter of the game is marked by an excessive number of minor and relatively trivial injuries exacerbated by the players' fatigue.

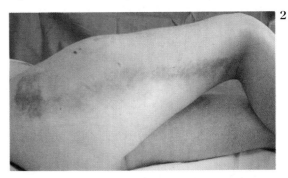

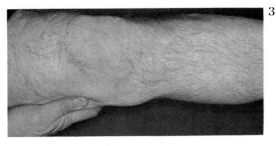

1 Sprain of the lateral collateral ligament of the ankle. A common injury too frequently badly treated.

2 Haematoma – an exaggerated example of a relatively common condition.

3 Anserine bursitis or 'breast-stroker's knee' – *not* common!

How different types of injury happen

Most injuries are accidental (though not always, **4**), and most overuse injuries may be considered incidental, almost to be expected in consequence of severe training loads. They can be readily classified by cause and fall into two major groups.

Extrinsic injuries are caused by forces generated outside the patient which can be due to a wide variety of situations, while intrinsic injuries are those caused by forces generated within the patient's own body. The injury may be direct, at the point of application of the force, or indirect when the damage occurs at a distance. It may be instantaneous or due to repeated subliminal stress or microtrauma, usually due to overuse. These injuries may give rise to a secondary (later) injury or other cause of diability.

Extrinsic injuries may be due to . . .

4 An accident?

5 Human violence, as in body-contact sports.

6 Accidents with apparatus or implements. The latter may be instantaneous or due to overuse.

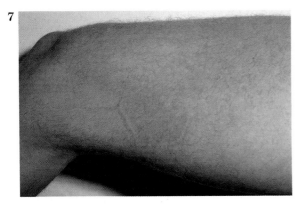

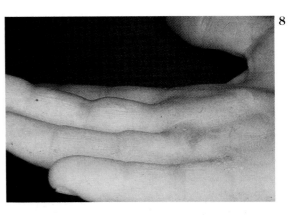

7 **Bruised thigh** showing the impact pattern of soccer ball.

8 **Callosity** overlying trigger finger in a fencer.

9 and **10** **Vehicular and environmental forces** also contribute to injury in sport.

Intrinsic injuries

Injuries may also be intrinsic – that is, due to forces generated within the patient. They may occur either spontaneously, as in a rupture of the long head of the biceps (**11**), or as a result of overuse – which may be acute as in tenosynovitis (**12**), or chronic as in fibrosing Achilles peritendonitis (**13**).

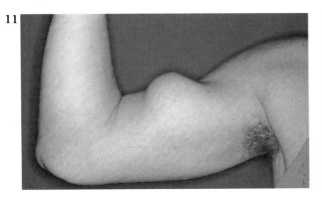

11 **Rupture** of the long head of the biceps.

12 **Tenosynovitis**, the result of acute overuse.

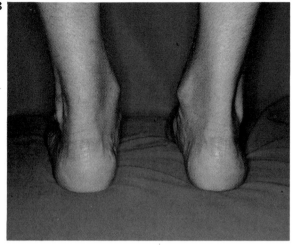

13 Achilles tendonitis in a long-distance runner, a chronic intrinsic overuse injury.

Generally, as would be expected, extrinsic injuries produce more severe tissue damage than intrinsic because the forces involved are substantially greater. In intrinsic injury the key causes are either breakdown of technique under stress (which leads to instantaneous injury) or the overlong or too great application of training loads or competition (which produces overuse injury). In the management of intrinsic injury, therefore, correction of any technical faults in the practice of the sport, with modification of the training programme, is an essential component of patient management.

In addition, continued participation while injured may provoke an immediate (but not necessarily related) second injury, which may lead on to reinjury or the development of early or late secondary conditions.

Secondary conditions

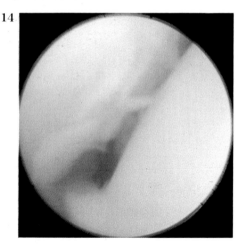

14 Chondromalacia patellae (arthroscopic appearance), an early secondary condition.

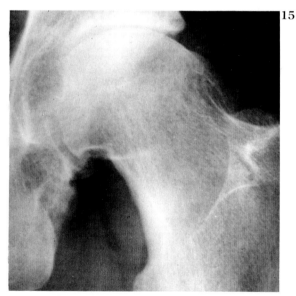

15 Osteoarthrosis of the hip in a race walker, a late secondary condition.

2 Types of tissue damage

Injury occurs when the body is unable to adapt to a force applied in the space/time continuum. Tissue response largely reflects the nature of the damaging mechanism, ie the manner in which the force is applied as well as its severity. The pattern of injury throughout the various tissues involved will tend to a degree of uniformity with some variation at individual sites as a response to peculiar local factors. The general pattern of tissue damage, however, remains reasonably constant throughout the body. Typical examples of pathological response to trauma in the tissues are repeatedly reproduced at different anatomical sites.

Skin injury

A variety of different types of trauma may be noted:
- **Laceration** is damage to the skin involving the full thickness and exposing the underlying subcutaneous tissue.
- **Abrasion or graze** is an injury, often of the glancing type, where the surface of the skin is broken but there is no complete tear through the whole depth.
- **Haematoma,** contusion or bruise is due to a direct blow on the surface, usually with a blunt instrument.
- **Puncture wounds** are lacerations where the depth of the wound is greater than its length or breadth. Typically they are the result of injury with a pointed instrument.
- **Burns** involve heat injury to the skin. In friction burns an abrasive component is invariably present as well.
- **Blisters** are injuries to the skin where one layer is detached from the layer beneath, the gap between becoming filled with a serous fluid exuded by the injured cells. (Blistering does not occur if the load is built up gradually, allowing the skin to adapt.)
- **Mixed injury** – for example, bruising and laceration together.

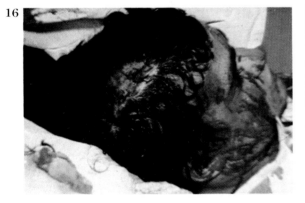

16 Scalp laceration through the full thickness of the skin, caused by the studs of a rugby boot.

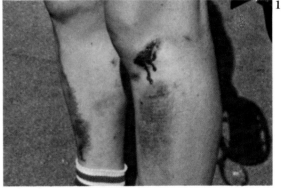

17 Abrasion due to direct violence – leg injuries to a cyclist after a fall in a road race.

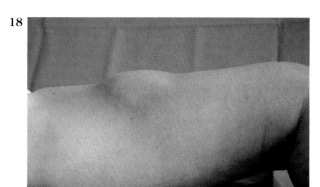

18 Haematoma from a blow from a field hockey ball.

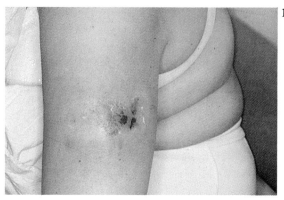

19 Crush and laceration – a bite from an angry horse.

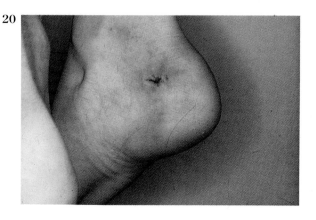

20 Puncture wound. An injury to the heel as a result of a bite from an irascible dog, suffered by a runner waylaid while out training. If a dog shows signs of aggression walk slowly. Don't run!

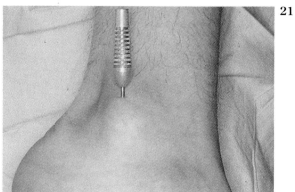

21 Puncture wound – off target!

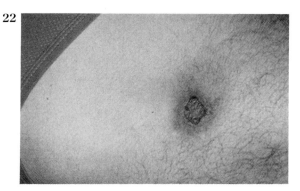

22 Grass burns. A friction burn on the skin of the thigh over the greater trochanter, caused by a sliding fall on hard ground. These burns commonly become secondarily infected.

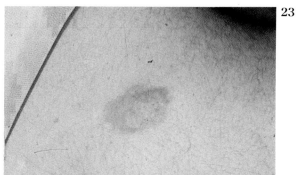

23 Hypertrophic scarring over the greater trochanter in a friction burn (in this case a cyclist fell during a track race) that healed with excessive scar-tissue formation.

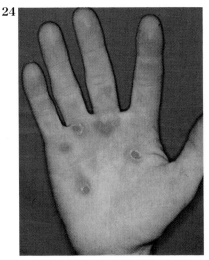

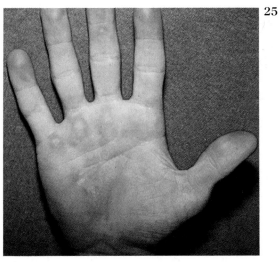

24 Blistered hands. As in other tissues, the response to overuse is injury – here in the form of blisters on the palms of an oarsman resuming training after a break.

25 Calloused palms. Provided the loading is built up gradually and progressively, tissues can adapt to high levels of use – callosities (seen here on the hands of an international gymnast) being one result.

Muscle injury/tear types

Muscle damage occurs either as a result of external forces (contusion, haematoma or laceration) or, more commonly, as the result of forces generated within the tissue, ie as an intrinsic injury. The injury is then called a strain or tear. There are three basic types: complete and partial, the latter being either insterstitial or intramuscular.

The severity of a muscle injury will depend very often on the degree of training of the individual. The fully fit athlete who is properly stretched before competing and who has an adequate technique will seldom become injured. In the fit subject bleeding is more marked but resolution subsequently more rapid. Chronic muscle tears invariably delay resumption of sport.

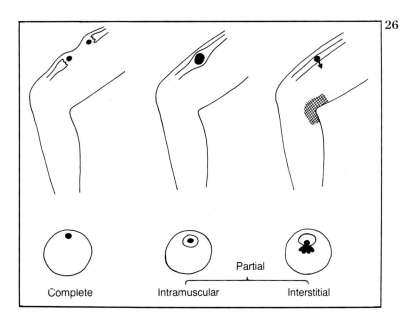

26 Types of muscle tear.

27 and **28 Action sequence of muscle tear.** The victim is the runner in the black strip.

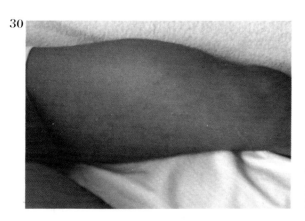

29 Complete rupture of the rectus femoris of a soccer player.

30 Intramuscular injury to another soccer player is indicated by the marked swelling of the quadriceps.

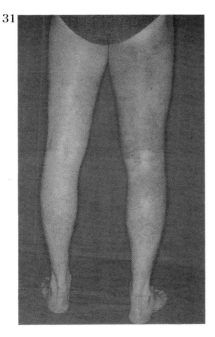

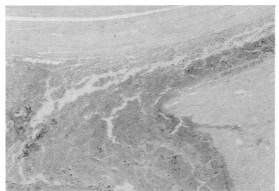

32 Muscle haematoma – histology.

31 Interstitial injury showing extravasation of blood – sprinter (hamstring injury).

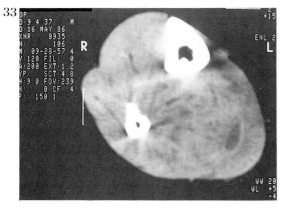

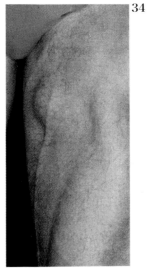

33 Cystic haematoma in gastrocnemius – appearance on CT scan.

34 Muscle hernia. Muscle tissue bulging up under pressure through a split in the overlying fascia (abductor). Probably an old interstitial tear.

35 and **36** **Loss of extensibility.** A recent injury of the right quadriceps, showing the normal side (**36**) – with the knee fully flexed and the hip fully extended – and the abnormal side (**35**) – the hip, here, is not fully extended, nor is the knee fully flexed.

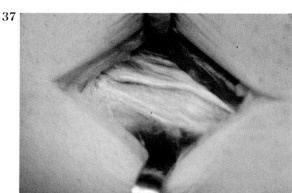

37 Muscle shortening (appearance at operation). Typically this is due to contraction of excess scar tissue in an inadequately treated partial tear (gastrocnemius).

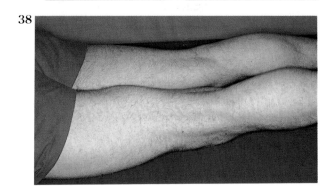

38 Muscle spasm (associated with joint injury). Note the apparent tightness in the hamstrings. This patient has sustained a knee injury and is unable to extend the knee fully. The appearance is due not to locking but rather to muscle spasm (not to be confused with muscle shortening associated with muscle injury).

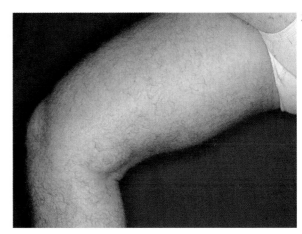

39 Muscle tear. In contrast to spasm, the mass in the muscle is palpable when the joint is flexed and the muscle contracts actively against resistance (in a spasm it is felt when the joint and muscle are *passively* stretched).

Ectopic calcification – myositis ossificans

This is a condition in which deposits of calcium and, eventually, bone are laid down in the muscle, usually as a result of a direct blow. As a rule it does not occur with intrinsic injury. It may be induced by overvigorous treatment (especially massage and passive stretching) of a muscle haematoma.

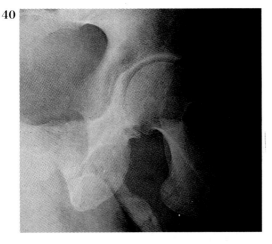

40 Ectopic calcification. An X-ray showing the well-defined bone formation in the adductor of a rugby player.

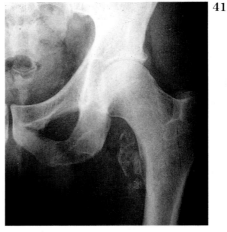

41 Ectopic calcification mimicked by a malignant tumour. This patient was sent for biopsy but was thought to be suffering from ectopic calcification in a torn adductor. The erosion of the cortex on the medial side is the give-away.

Myositis ossificans

A blow on the front of the thigh suffered by a young soccer player has led to the quadriceps being affected by myositis ossificans – whose development and resolution are shown in the series of X-rays reproduced below. Note the time span for resolution.

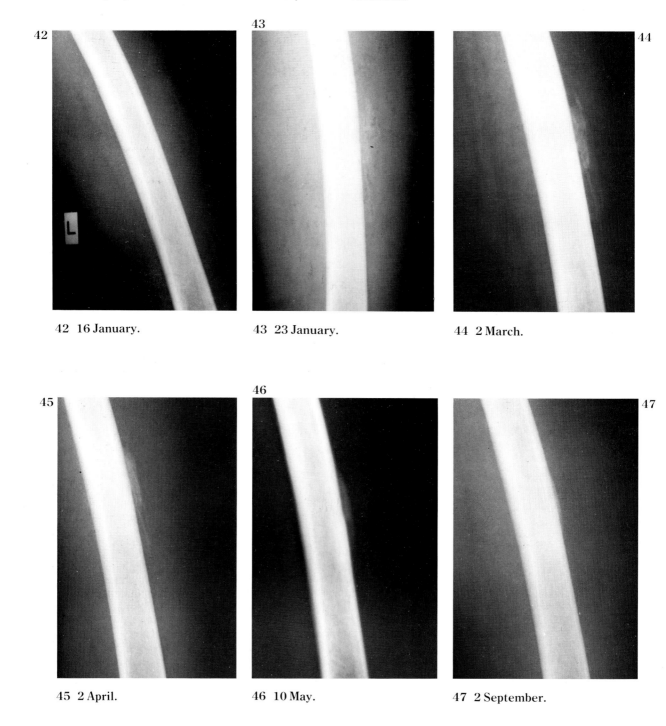

42 16 January.

43 23 January.

44 2 March.

45 2 April.

46 10 May.

47 2 September.

48 Ectopic bone (operation specimen). After removal of the ectopic bone, the individual was able to resume playing rugby football.

49 Ectopic calcification or myositis ossificans – histological appearance.

Tendon injury

Damage to tendons by direct violence in sport is uncommon. Usually injuries are intrinsic and most are of the overuse type. They are readily classified by their local pathology which is associated with well-defined clinical features.

Diagnosis	Key features
Rupture – complete	Sudden onset Gap in tendon
Rupture – partial	Sudden onset No gap in tendon
Focal degeneration	Gradual onset Well-localized tenderness Minimal swelling Moves with tendon
Tendonitis	Gradual onset Diffuse tenderness Well-marked swelling Moves with tendon
Peritendonitis – acute	Rapid onset Crepitus Diffuse swelling Does not move with tendon
Peritendonitis – chronic	Slow onset – often with repeated episodes Localized thickening Does not move with tendon
Mixed lesion	Mixed features

50 Classification of types of tendon lesion and key clinical features.

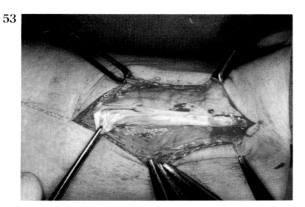

51 Sites of lesions.

SITES

Supraspinatus
Biceps Brachii Long Head
Wrist Extensors
Thumb Extensors
Finger Flexors
Iliotibial Band
Biceps Femoris Tendon
Patellar Tendon
Achilles Tendon
Extensor Retinaculum
Peronei
Posterior Tibial Tendons

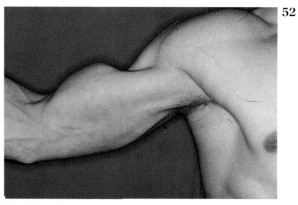

52 Complete tendon rupture (long head of biceps). The tendon ends are separated by the pull of the attached muscle which becomes virtually non-functional.

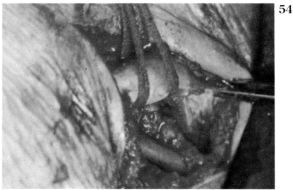

53 Partial tendon rupture (Achilles tendon). Muscle function is not mechanically impaired as a rule but is inhibited by pain.

54 Focal degeneration with calcification (tibialis posterior tendon). Clinically and functionally this is similar to partial rupture, of which it is the overuse variant.

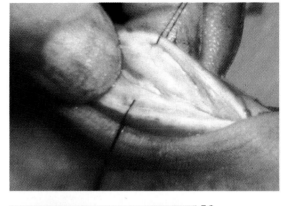

55 Tendonitis (Achilles tendon). Generalized oedema and inflammation of the tendon causing variable pain and loss of function.

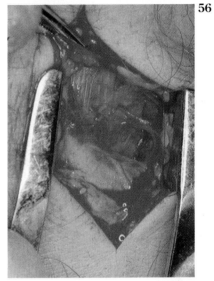

56 Peritendonitis (patellar tendon). This is an overuse injury characterized initially by oedema and later by fibrosis in tissues surrounding the tendon. It may be acute or chronic. Adhesion to surrounding structures is common.

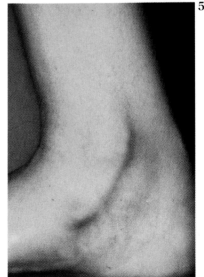

57 Tendovaginitis (tibialis posterior). Usually a chronic inflammation with fibrosis and stenosis of the tendon sheath.

Joint injury

Joint injuries are common in sport, particularly in body-contact events. The range of damage varies from minor sprain to major fracture or dislocation. Most joints are synovial, being reinforced in certain sites by ligaments, and some contain fibro-cartilaginous menisci. Any or all of these structures may be damaged. Traumatic synovitis occurs as the result of joint injury in which the lining membrane or synovium is affected. Where the damage is severe the response is acute and haemorrhagic, where damage is less severe the response is a serous effusion.

Traumatic synovitis

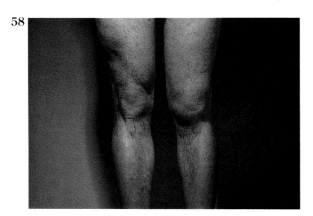

58 Clinical appearance of traumatic synovitis showing swelling and effusion in the left knee after a rugby injury.

	Synovial effusion	Haemarthrosis
Onset	Delayed ± 12 hours	Immediate
Tension	Usually slight	Considerable
Volume	Usually small (50 ml –)	Large (50 ml +)
Severity of injury	+ → ++	++ → +++ ++

59 Differential diagnosis in joint effusion. Note that in very severe injury, capsular disruption may allow escape of haemarthrosis into surrounding tissues.

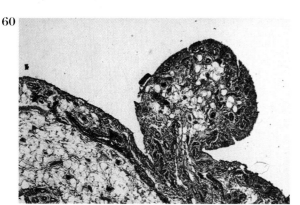

60 Low grade traumatic synovitis – histology of villus.

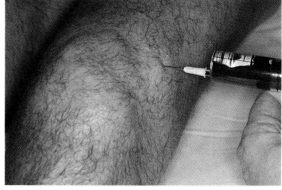

61 Haemarthrosis – aspiration of blood-stained synovial fluid from the knee of a soccer player. This procedure must only be carried out in hygienic conditions. Formal shaving, draping and scrub up is not necessary provided the skin is cleaned and a no-touch technique is used.

Loose bodies

Loose bodies are a common cause of joint problems in sport, usually because they interfere mechanically with the function of the joint. In some instances, as in osteochondritis dissecans, discomfort in the joint may be associated with the underlying condition.

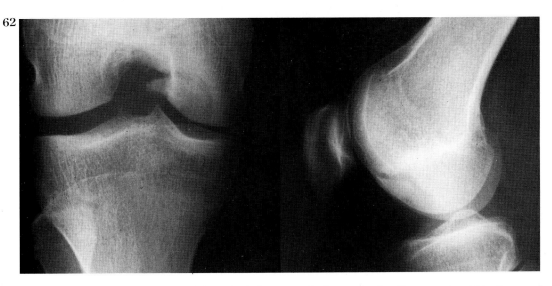

62 Osteochondritis dissecans. A loose body is commonly the result of earlier osteochondritis dissecans; in this case, the medial femoral condyle is involved.

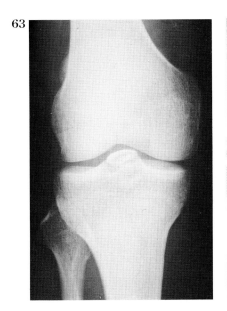

63 Loose body caused by an old fracture of the anterior tibial spine.

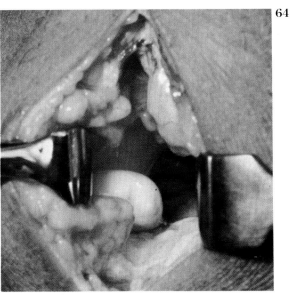

64 Loose body demonstrated at operation, removed because it was causing locking. Unless very large, such bodies are usually readily removed arthroscopically.

65

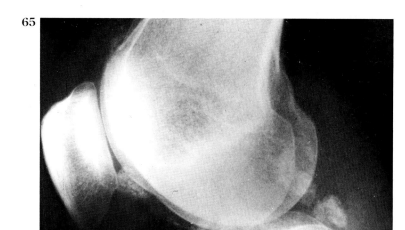

65 Osteochondromatosis (synovial chondromatosis). Multiple loose bodies.

66

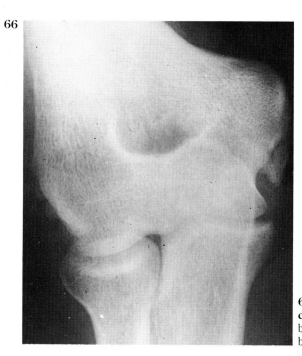

66 Golfer's elbow (capsular calcification). The condition must not be confused with intra-capsular loose body.

67

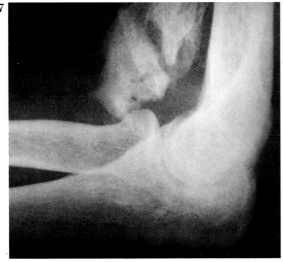

67 Ectopic calcification. Abnormal bone deposits on the anterior aspect of the elbow joint, superficial but attached to the capsule.

Ligament injury

Damage to ligaments may cause minor tears, stretching or complete rupture. Complete rupture leads to mechanical instability, while tearing – even if quite minor – may damage the proprioceptive feedback mechanism and lead to 'stable instability'.

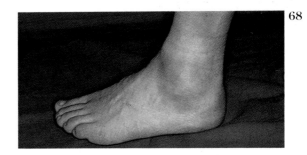

68

68 Sprain. A traction injury to a ligament without loss of continuity.

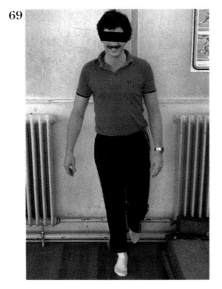

69

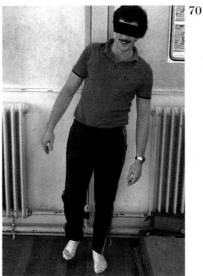

70

69 and **70 'Stable instability'.** Loss of proprioception in the left ankle joint as a result of ligament injury with no gross mechanical instability. The normal side (**69**) is shown for comparison. Note the patient's inability to balance properly on the affected ankle (**70**). This modified Romberg's sign is elicited with the patient's eyes *closed*.

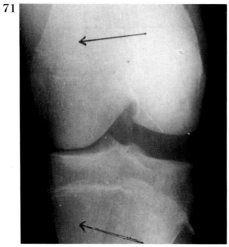

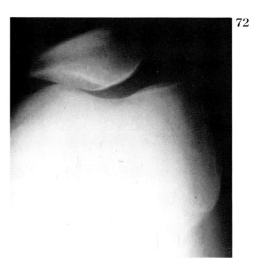

71 Ligament rupture with loss of continuity and mechanical instability.

72 Subluxation. Misalignment of joint surface, but some overlap.

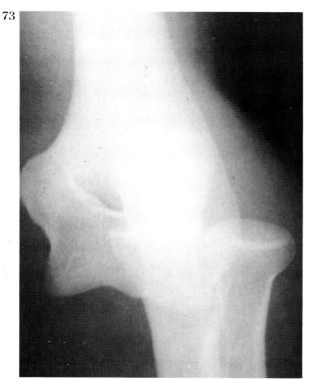

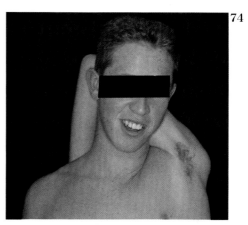

74 Hypermobility. Excessive laxity or 'double-jointedness' may be so severe as to be pathological, and is a contraindication to body-contact sports and those requiring excess mobility (eg, gymnastics and trampolining), especially in children.

73 Dislocation. Complete disruption of joint surface contact.

Dislocation is often associated with severe ligamentous injury leading to instability. In some cases, particularly around the elbow joint, damage leads during the recovery phase to ectopic calcification and subsequent limitation in joint function.

Vascular injury

Vascular injury usually complicates other injury but is occasionally isolated. These conditions generally occur as a result of a direct blow or wound. Spontaneous arterial thrombosis has been described but is probably due to intimal damage. Later aneurysm or arteriovenous fistula may form.

Venous thrombosis is much more common, often associated with an episode of overuse. No specific sites are particularly implicated but the lower limb is more usually involved. Congenital anomalies (eg, compression due to cervical rib) or vascular tumours may present in, or have their effects exacerbated by, sport.

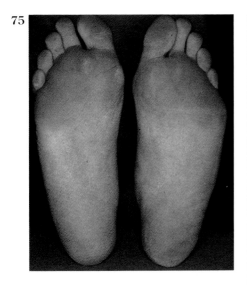

75 Deep vein thrombosis in the plantar veins of the foot (due to unaccustomed exercise on a very hard floor surface).

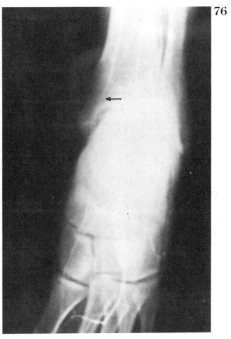

76 Traumatic thrombosis of the dorsalis pedis artery in a soccer player.

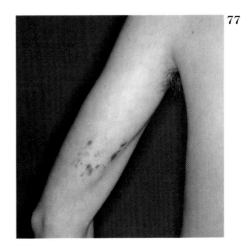

77 Cavernous haemangioma presenting due to pain associated with swimming.

Nerve injury

The commonest type of nerve injury is neuropraxia caused by a direct blow, eg over the ulnar nerve at the elbow or the lateral popliteal nerve at the fibula neck. More severe damage may complicate lacerations (division of nerve) and fractures and dislocations. Overuse injury is rare but includes ulnar neuritis in throwers. The most usual sites are illustrated below.

78

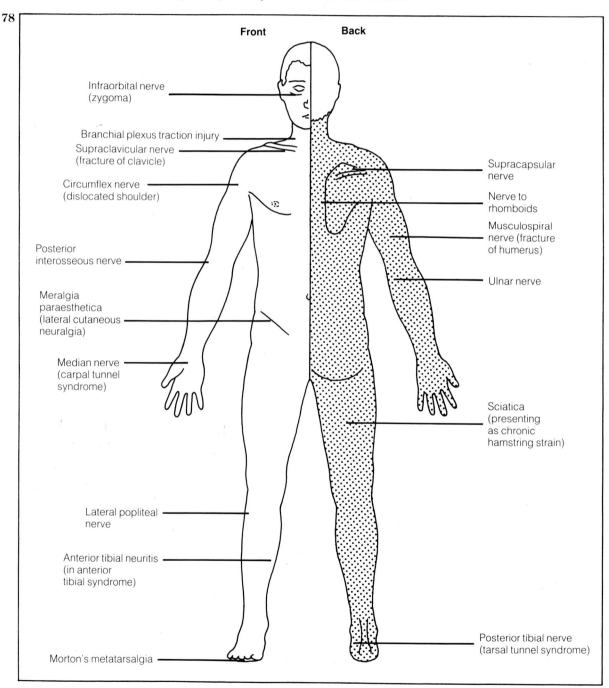

Front

Back

Infraorbital nerve (zygoma)

Branchial plexus traction injury

Supraclavicular nerve (fracture of clavicle)

Circumflex nerve (dislocated shoulder)

Posterior interosseous nerve

Meralgia paraesthetica (lateral cutaneous neuralgia)

Median nerve (carpal tunnel syndrome)

Lateral popliteal nerve

Anterior tibial neuritis (in anterior tibial syndrome)

Morton's metatarsalgia

Supracapsular nerve

Nerve to rhomboids

Musculospiral nerve (fracture of humerus)

Ulnar nerve

Sciatica (presenting as chronic hamstring strain)

Posterior tibial nerve (tarsal tunnel syndrome)

78 Common sites of nerve injury caused in sport.

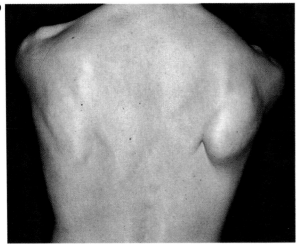

79 Rhomboid palsy – here due to viral infection.

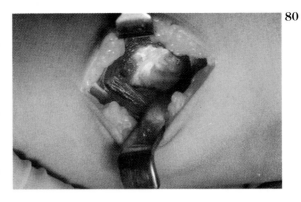

80 Posterior interosseous nerve entrapment – appearance at operative decompression. A cause of 'tennis elbow' symptoms.

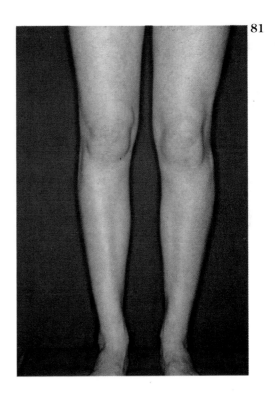

81 Abnormal fibula head associated with lateral popliteal neuritis.

Bone injury

Bone injuries are quite common in sport, usually as a result of direct violence (sometimes deliberate!). Generally, fractures sustained in sport differ little from those sustained in other activities. Treatment may have to be more vigorous, particularly during the rehabilitation phase, and in some instances internal fixation may be the treatment of choice to diminish the disability period.

Instantaneous fracture

82 A soccer player breaks his leg.

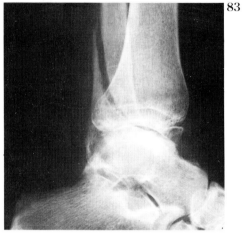

83 **Fractured fibula** in a soccer accident. Note also impingement exostosis on the anterior tibial joint margin.

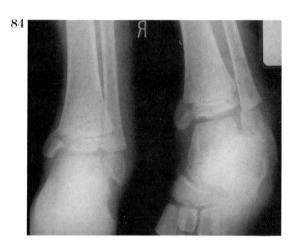

84 **Fractures involving ununited epiphyses** may cause distortion in later life and should be closely followed up.

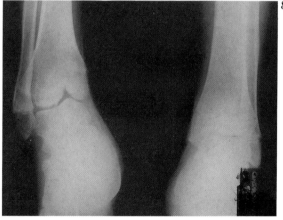

85 **Case 84 four years later.** Distortion of lower tibia with deformity of the ankle following fracture interfering with the distal tibial epiphysis.

Subchondral fracture

Occasionally there may be bony damage beneath the articular cartilage (a common site is the knee), associated either with ligament injury or with the presence of a loose body jamming between the joint surfaces. Diagnosis is often problematical as the defect may be extremely difficult to pick up radiologically.

Osteoid osteoma

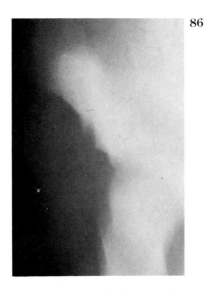

86 Osteoid osteoma in ilium. Such a lesion (uncommon) may be confused with a stress fracture.

Pathological fracture

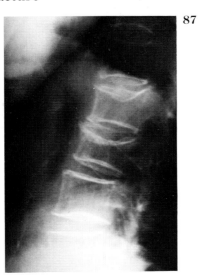

87 Wedge fracture in osteoporosis. This elderly patient tripped on a bowling green.

Stress fracture

Stress fractures of the tibia, fibula and metatarsals are very common in sport as a result of excessive training on hard surfaces.

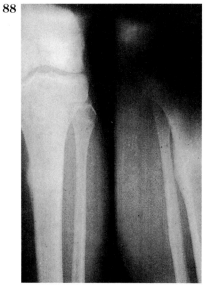

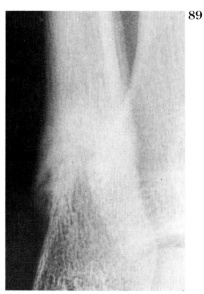

88 Stress fracture of tibia.

89 Stress fracture of fibula.

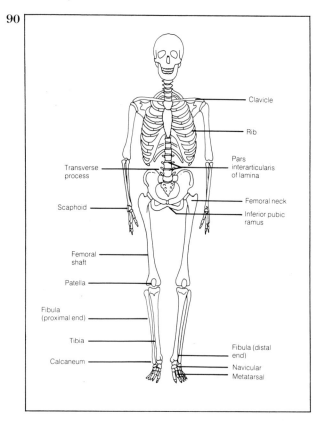

90 Usual sites of stress fractures in sportsmen.

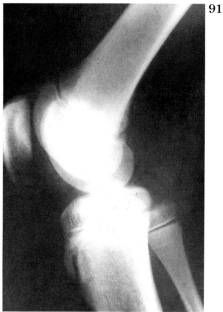

91 Osteochondritis or epiphysitis is more common in children. Osgood-Schlatter's disease – a traction stress epiphysitis.

3 Other conditions presenting as sports injuries

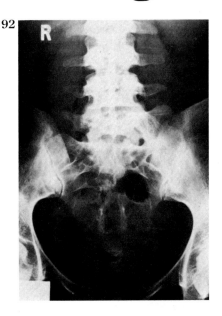

92

Congenital abnormalities may cause problems, particularly in the very active, and may present as injury, or cause injury.

92 Congenital asymmetric lumbosacral anomaly associated with pain in an equestrian.

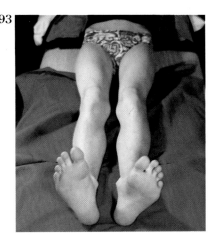

93

93 Torsion of the tibia. Misalignment of foot and knee causes problems to the enthusiastic runner.

Inflammation

Inflammatory disease may present as pain first felt during sport. Ankylosing spondylitis, Reiter's syndrome and rheumatoid arthritis regularly affect sportsmen.

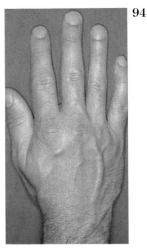

94

94 Rheumatoid disease. This golfer complained of small joint pains in the hands after a round of golf. He proved to have sero-positive rheumatoid disease.

Infection

Infections may appear as sports injuries. The patient presents having first experienced pain in the affected tissue during sporting activity (when local blood supply is greater than at rest).

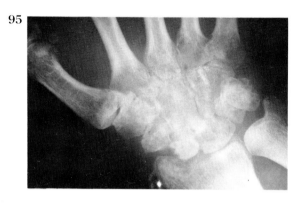

95 Septic arthritis. Radiograph of the wrist of an international athlete with septic arthritis. After treatment he was able to return to international competition. Note the severe decalcification.

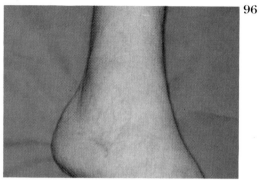

96 Acute osteomyelitis in the lower end of the fibula in a young rugby player. Initial presentation suggested a stress fracture – note the swelling over the lateral malleolus.

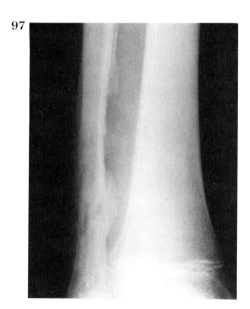

97 The X-ray appearance of 96 one month after onset. The patient has now returned to active sport with no disability.

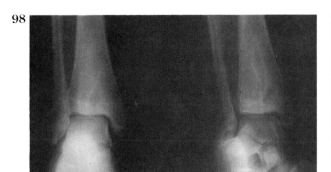

98

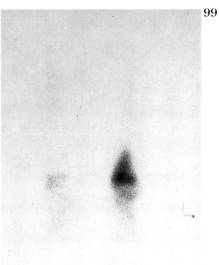

99

98 Chronic non-suppurative osteomyelitis. This young rugby player experienced persistent pain over several months, worse at night and with exercise, but the lower leg showed none of the cardinal signs of inflammation. The plain X-ray revealed minimal sclerosis and no evidence of sequestrum.

99 The radionucleide scan of 98 shows a classical 'hot node'.

Tumours

Tumours may present as sports injuries.

Benign tumours

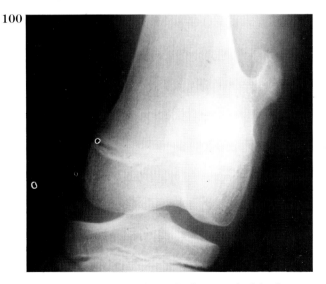

100

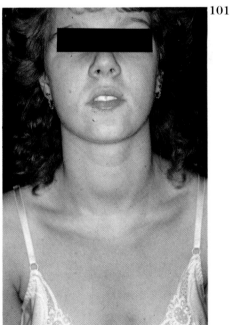

101

100 Solitary exostosis on the lower end of the femur interfering with vastus medialis function in a young swimmer.

101 This tumour moved with swallowing – a goitre! The patient presented with shortness of breath on exertion.

Borderline cases

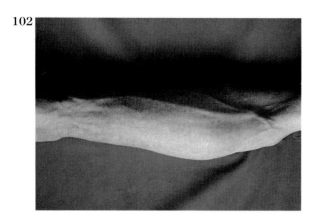

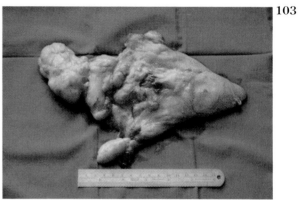

102 and **103** **Lipoma** with some primitive cells previously diagnosed as a 'muscle tear' in an angler.

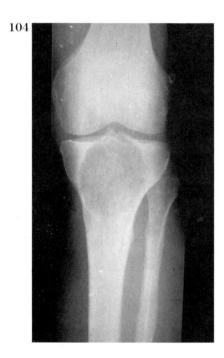

104 Giant cell tumour – an X-ray of the upper end of the tibia.

Malignant tumours

Malignant connective tissue tumours are uncommon but prognosis tends to be bad so that early detection is essential to reduce mortality rate. The possibility that a malignant tumour may present as a sports injury should always be remembered. A high index of suspicion will lead to early diagnosis and perhaps the avoidance of tragedy.

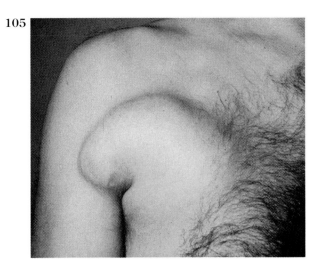

105 Rhabdomyosarcoma of the pectoralis major.

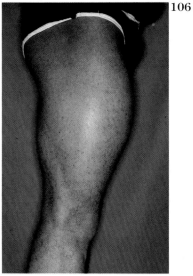

106 Intramuscular tear? This patient presented with acute onset of pain in the quadriceps on exertion and was diagnosed as having an intramuscular tear. However, he did not improve rapidly with treatment and the swelling subsequently increased. This was later shown to be haemorrhage into a rhabdomyosarcoma.

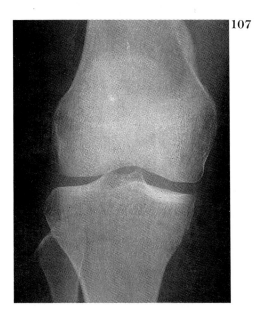

107 X-ray showing osteosarcoma in the femur of a schoolgirl, presenting as pain in the knee after netball.

4 Head and facial injuries

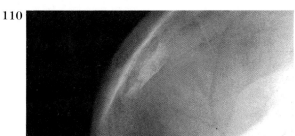

Head injury

Head injuries are too common. They involve transient dazing, or periods of unconsciousness with more or less severe brain damage. They occur in body-contact and vehicular sports and in hard-ball games. Adequate headgear may not fully protect. Emergency resuscitation may be needed.

Even mild cases of concussion should be treated. The 10-second rule should apply in all sports.

After head injury, supervised observation is mandatory. No player who has been concussed should be allowed home unaccompanied. Significant loss of consciousness demands proper hospitalization and follow-up. Return to sport should be gradual and delayed. The possibility of late sequelae, eg subdural haematoma, must never be forgotten.

108 Transient dazing is common. Patients usually respond well to a cold douche.

109 Concussion may occur when there are heavy impacts in body-contact sport, eg in a clash of heads.

110 Skull fracture. A golf ball can be a dangerous missile – as this X-ray of a victim of a golf ball injury, showing a depressed fracture of the skull, indicates.

111 Protective headgear. Even adequate headgear may not protect entirely from a blow to the head.

112 Severe concussion with unconsciousness will require vigorous resuscitation.

Eye injury

Too many eye injuries occur in sport even when protection is worn. They vary in severity from the corneal abrasion or subconjunctival haemorrhage to disruption of the eyeball, and some are due to deliberate violence. All eye injuries should be regarded as serious and referred for specialist attention.

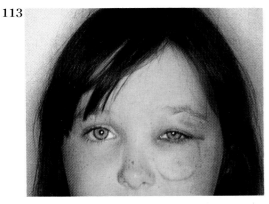

113 Facial injury due to a blow from a tennis ball – the patient was wearing glasses.

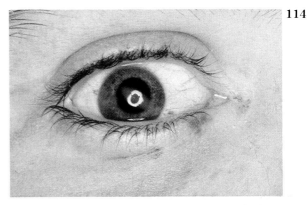

114 Corneal abrasion – stained with fluorescein dye.

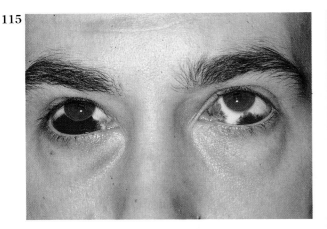

115 Subconjunctival haemorrhage. Looks dramatic but is not usually serious.

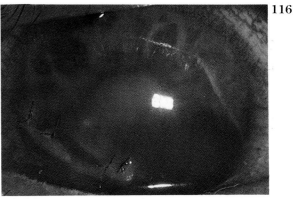

116 Hyphaema. Blood in the anterior chamber from a blow from a squash ball.

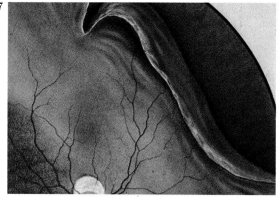

117 Retinal detachment. A real risk in the myope in body-contact sport.

Facial injury

Injury to the face occurs mostly in body-contact sports, particularly in those events where face guards are not worn. As a rule, except in high-velocity vehicular injuries, damage is relatively slight, though the vulnerability of the eye, the teeth and the jaw must not be forgotton. In sports involving implements or missiles – for example, in ice hockey, lacrosse or cricket – facial protection may be necessary.

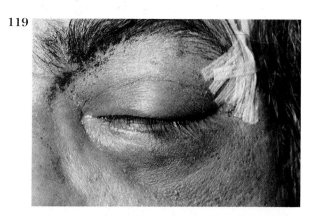

118 'Cut eye'. A supraorbital laceration in a soccer player.

119 Haematoma of the eye – a 'black eye'. This particular injury was associated with a fractured zygoma.

120 Facial injury is always a risk when the rules are forgotten and tempers lost.

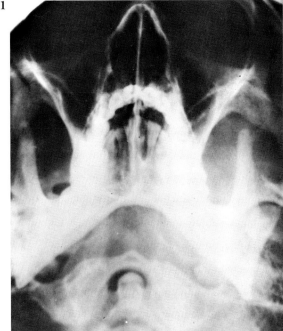

121 Fracture of zygoma. A not-uncommon injury after a fight in a rugby match.

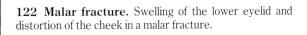

122 Malar fracture. Swelling of the lower eyelid and distortion of the cheek in a malar fracture.

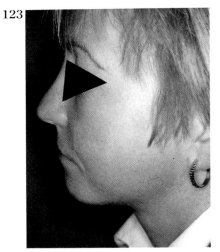

123 Facial swelling due to surgical emphysema in a maxillary fracture.

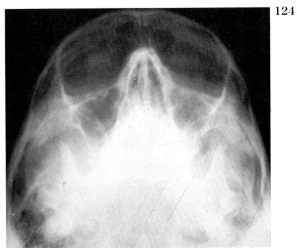

124 X-ray of 123.

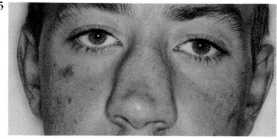

125 Fractured nasal bone. This is almost invariably caused by combat body-contact sports such as boxing or judo.

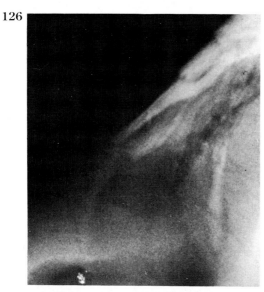

126 An X-ray of the nasal fracture in 125.

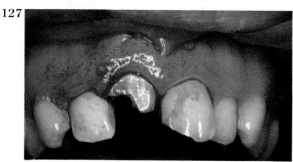

127 Dental injury. Teeth broken by direct violence. The wearing of mouth guards will prevent such damage and is particularly recommended in rugby football and boxing.

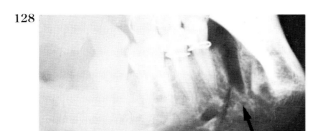

128 X-ray of mandibular fracture. Note the empty tooth socket.

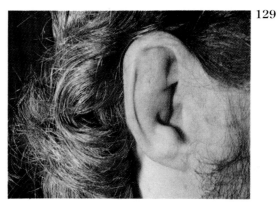

129 Haematoma of auricle – 'cauliflower ear'. In the acute phase, evacuation of the haematoma and compression dressing may prevent the typical deformity of the ear. Protection is given by wearing a scrum cap or by binding adhesive tape around the head to cover the ears.

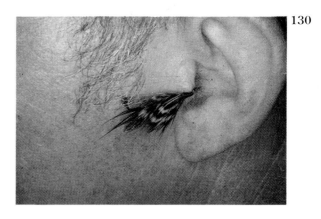

130 'Foul-hooked'!

5 Neck injuries

Cervical spine

Congenital abnormalities

Congenital abnormalities of the cervical spine are relatively unimportant and are often incidental findings. However, relative impairment of normal function produced by these conditions may be sufficient to interfere with sporting activity. When some specific potential weakness is present, sport may be competely contraindicated.

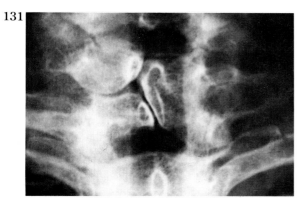

131 Cervical spina bifida occulta, an anteroposterior X-ray.

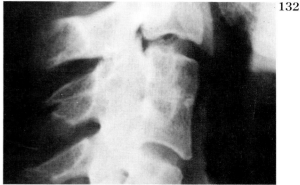

132 Congenital fusion of the 3rd and 4th cervical vertebrae, a lateral X-ray. This is a minor variant of the Klippel-Feil syndrome.

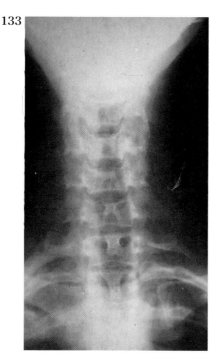

Patients presenting with cervical symptoms in whom these types of conditions are found should be cautioned away from neck-stressing sports, ie soccer and rugby, trampolining and gymnastics, judo and wrestling.

133 Cervical ribs, an anteroposterior X-ray. This condition is associated with interference with function of the distal root of the brachial plexus and the subclavian artery. It is the interference with function that brings the patient in for treatment.

Injuries

Fortunately, injuries of the cervical spine are relatively uncommon. However, because of the vulnerability of the spinal cord, the consequences where they do occur can be tragic. Therefore, potential danger situations must be recognized and, where feasible, factors liable to cause injury – for example, the spearing tackle in American football – must be banned. Cervical cord damage is always a possibility where sport-related – particularly *body-contact* sport-related – injuries are concerned. It is important, therefore, that adequate first aid and resuscitation facilities are available at fixtures such as rugby matches where the chances of sustaining such injuries are greatest.

Danger situations

134 The rugby scrummage collapses. Note the position of the arrowed player.

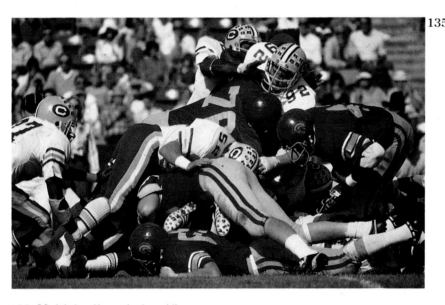

135 Multiple pile-up in the gridiron game.

136 Diving into shallow water, particularly if the bottom cannot be seen easily.

In these examples – as in other danger situations – it is forced flexion with rotation (less commonly forced hyperextension) that usually does the damage. Rigid control by referees and self-control by players will reduce the hazard. Risk situations should if possible be removed from the sport, if necessary by changing the rules.

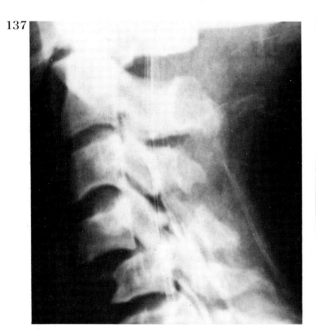

137 Dislocation. A lateral X-ray showing dislocation at C 4/5 (a diving accident). This type of injury is usually associated with gross neurological damage leading to tetraplegia. Bad handling could convert a case with no neurological damage to a tetraplegic.

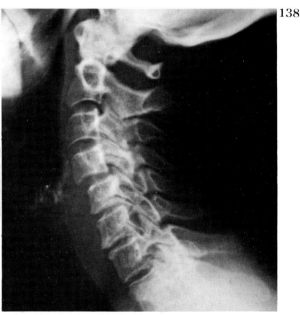

138 Subluxation. A lateral X-ray showing subluxation at C 4/5 (a riding accident). This type of injury may be associated with transient neurological damage. The patient often complains of symptoms related to the local nerve roots.

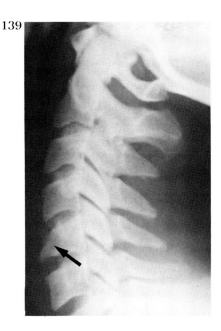

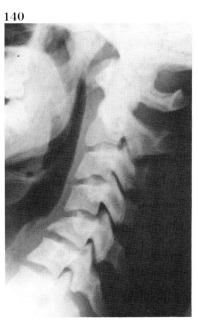

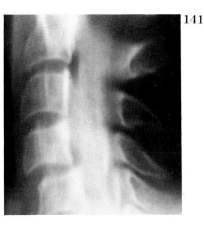

141 (In forced flexion) narrowing of spinal canal.

This patient, a teenage junior rugby international, was experiencing minimal symptoms only. Nevertheless, an injury of this type inevitably means a complete ban on playing rugby or any other neck-stressing sports.

139 (In extension) deformity of C 5 vertebral body.

140 (In flexion) forward subluxation of C 4.

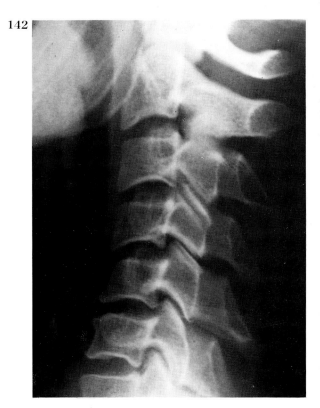

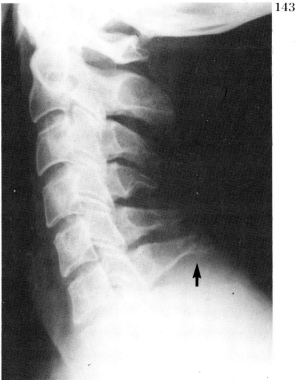

142 Loss of normal cervical contour due to muscle spasm in a rugby forward. Neurological signs are unusual but root pain is commonly a symptom due to inflammation of the posterior facetal joints.

143 Fracture of spinous process of C 6. Injury to a rugby forward due to indirect violence, the pull of the muscles on the ligamentum nuchae.

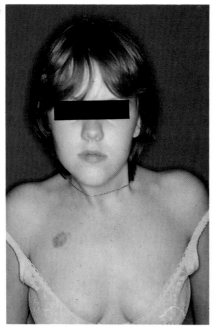

144   **Acute spasmodic torticollis** in a young gymnast after a fall while vaulting.

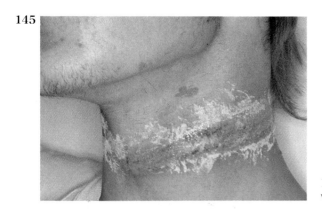

145   **Rope burn on the neck** of a motorcycle trialist who ran off the circuit into a boundary rope.

Happily, most spinal injuries in sport are relatively minor, although occasionally and tragically severe injury with spinal cord damage occurs. Where causative factors can be clearly identified – for example, in swimming (diving into shallow water) and in rugby (deliberate collapsing of the scrum) – every attempt should be made both by persuasion and by coercion to eliminate dangerous activities. In all cases of doubt, the possibility of spinal cord damage with all its consequences must be considered. The patient must be handled with utmost caution.

6 Shoulder and arm injuries

Clavicle

The clavicle – the strut on which the shouder is braced out from the trunk – is frequently injured in sport.

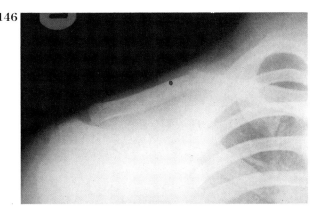

146 Greenstick fracture of the clavicle in a schoolboy.

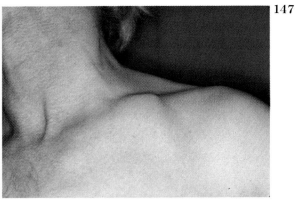

147 Typical appearance of clavicular fracture with obvious bone deformity.

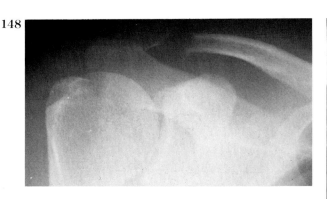

148 Clavicular fracture – an unusual site with subsequent separation.

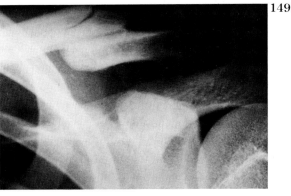

149 Refracture – the result of a young judoka returning to his sport too soon. Consolidation must be well advanced before sport is resumed, particularly if bone-end apposition is poor.

Inadequate and casual management of clavicular fractures leads to non-union, or mal-union with overlap and shortening of the clavicular strut leading to malfunction of the shoulder.

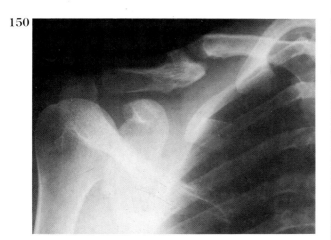

150

150 Non-union in an inadequately treated clavicular fracture.

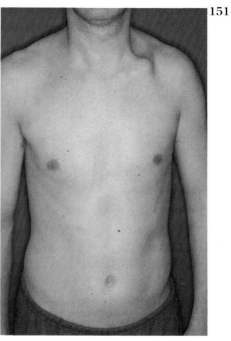

151

151 Distortion of the shoulder due to clavicular fracture healing with gross overlap.

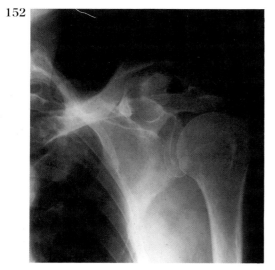

152

152 **Mal-union** in a clavicular fracture with a mass of ectopic calcification.

153

153 A fall from a horse. Clavicular and shoulder injuries commonly follow a fall from a horse.

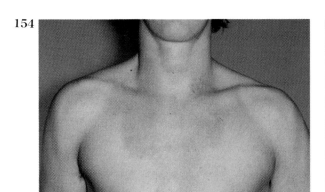

154 Sternoclavicular subluxation – clinical appearance. A relatively unusual condition difficult to treat if the joint becomes clinically unstable.

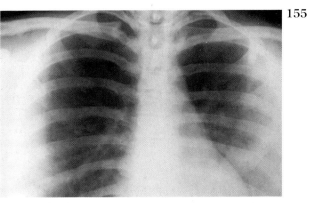

155 Sternoclavicular subluxation showing increase in joint gap demonstrated radiographically.

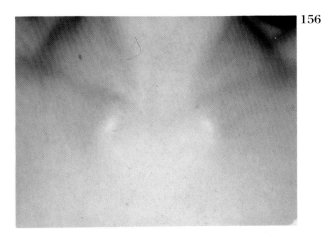

156 Teitze's disease. This is not trauma but a (usually) monarticular inflammatory disease affecting typically sternocostal rather than sternoclavicular joints.

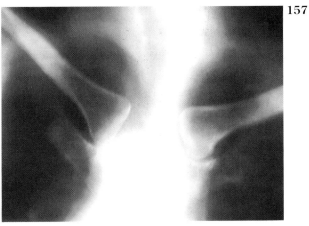

157 Tomogram showing ectopic calcification in the intra-articular disc in the sternoclavicular joint.

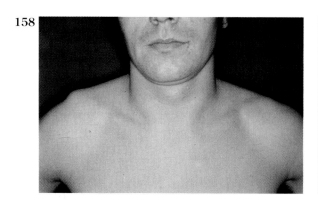 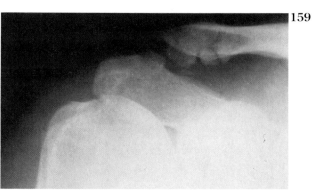

158 Acromioclavicular subluxation – clinical appearance. A common injury due to a fall on the point of the shoulder. The deformity is obvious.

159 Acromioclavicular subluxation – an X-ray showing separation but not wide distraction. Note also the damage to outer end of the clavicle – this is a rugby injury.

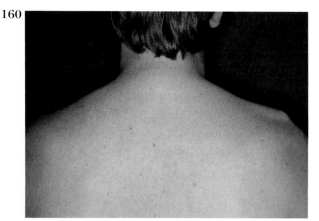 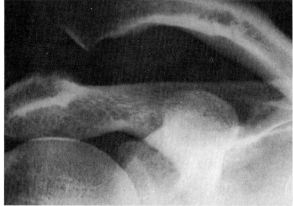

160 Acromioclavicular dislocation. The deformity is similar to that in subluxation but much more marked (as would be expected), and the displacement reduces on downward pressure on the clavicle.

161 Dislocation of the acromioclavicular joint with rupture of the conoid and trapezoid ligaments with wide distraction of the joint surfaces. This severe injury demands surgical repair for effective restoration of shoulder function.

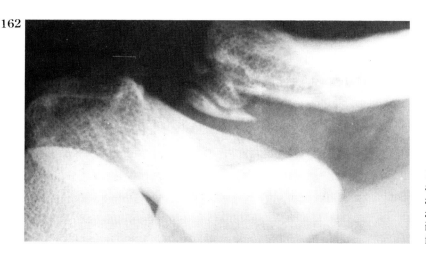

162 Ectopic calcification in acromioclavicular injury – X-ray appearance. This condition is associated with repeated capsular injury, in this case to a rugby league footballer.

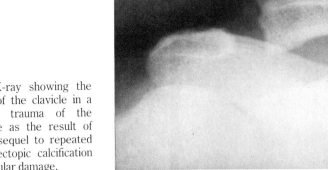

163 Traumatic osteolysis. An X-ray showing the cystic appearance of the outer end of the clavicle in a patient sustaining repeated minor trauma of the acromioclavicular joint – in this case as the result of playing rugby. This is probably the sequel to repeated articular cartilage damage whereas ectopic calcification (**162**) is associated with repeated capsular damage.

Scapula

Fractures of the scapula occur uncommonly in sport and, although frequently painful, are not usually serious.

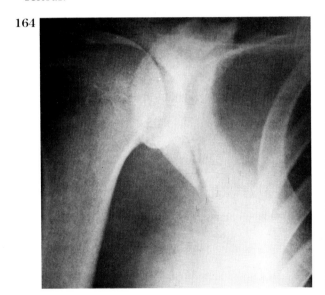

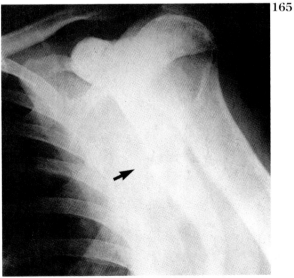

164 Fracture of the wing of the scapula just medial to the glenoid in a young county rugby player.

165 Fracture of the whole blade of the scapula. Treatment of these injuries is essentially symptomatic with relief of pain and early mobilization as the object.

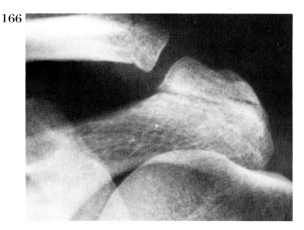

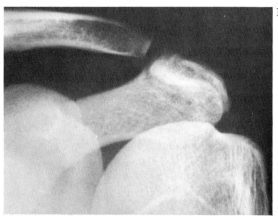

166 Fracture of the acromion in a footballer after a charge tackle. *Note:* there is a fracture of the outer end of the clavicle as well. In some views there may appear to be a fracture of the acromion, but this is an artefact due to projection (unless a break in the cortical margin is shown as well).

167 Acromial abnormality in a young javelin thrower. In this case an ununited ossification centre is present in the outer end of the acromion. This is abnormal – not pathological.

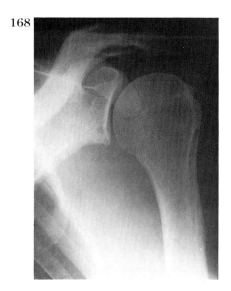

168 Fracture of the inferior margin of the glenoid. An unusual injury caused by a fall on the side of the shoulder with the arm abducted (clutching a football).

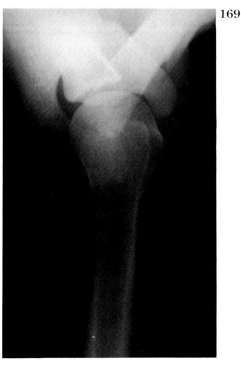

169 Coracoid fracture – due to avulsion force of brachialis and long head of biceps.

Soft-tissue injuries around the scapula are relatively uncommon and may cause diagnostic uncertainty. Note that some sportspersons (eg, tennis players) often display asymmetric muscular development.

Muscle tears usually occur when the muscle concerned is acting as a prime mover and the movement is forcibly blocked.

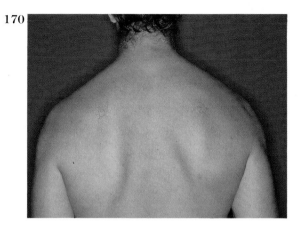

170 Asymmetric muscle development in a bow side oarsman.

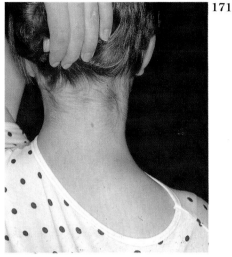

171 Trapezius tear in a table-tennis player who caught the bat on the table attempting a top spin smash.

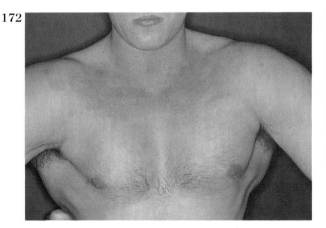

172 Pectoralis major insertion avulsion in a body builder.

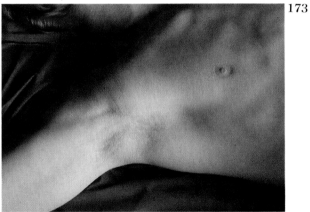

173 Old partial rupture of pectoralis major with interstitial scarring. The true nature of this case only came to light on examination under general anaesthetic.

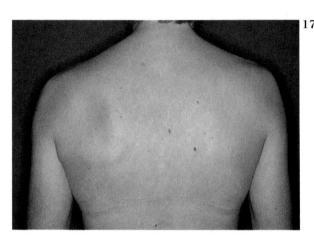

174 Rupture of supraspinatus in a power lifter – sudden onset in attempting a snatch.

175 *Not* **a muscle rupture!** Wasting of infraspinatus in suprascapular nerve palsy – of insidious onset.

Shoulder joint

Shoulder joint injuries are particularly common in sport. They may be the result of overuse, as in racket games such as badminton and tennis, or the result of throwing or bowling as in cricket. Alternatively, they may occur by direct violence, either in body-contact sport, such as rugby union and league football, or as the result of a fall.

Generally, the clinical picture is similar to shoulder injuries in other activities. Because the shoulder joint is so dependent on soft tissues for its stability, injuries to these structures are common and tend to become chronic. Disability is often out of proportion to the extent of the tissue damage.

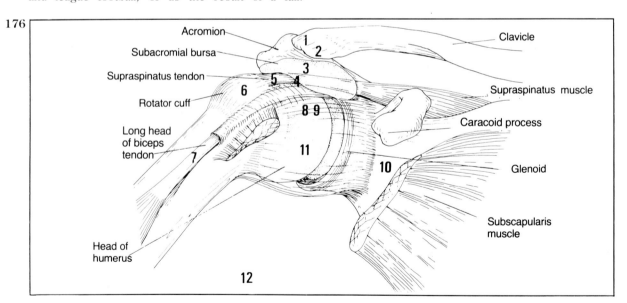

176 Shoulder pain – the differential diagnosis.

KEY		
	1 Acromioclavicular sprain/subluxation/dislocation /osteoarthrosis/bursitis	7 Bicipital tendovaginitis
	2 Traumatic osteolysis, lateral end of clavicle	8 Capsulitis of shoulder joint
	3 Subacromial bursitis	9 'Frozen shoulder'
	4 Supraspinatus tendonitis	10 Recurrent subluxation/dislocation
	5 Supraspinatus ⎫ calcification rupture	11 Osteoarthrosis
	6 Rotator cuff ⎭	12 Referred pain

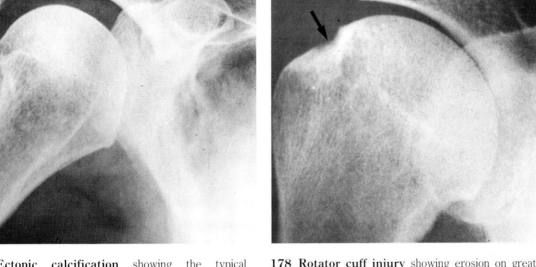

177 Ectopic calcification showing the typical appearance of calcium deposit: supraspinatus tendon.

178 Rotator cuff injury showing erosion on greater tuberosity.

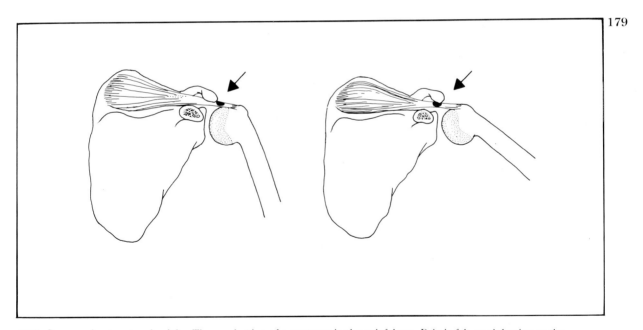

179 Supraspinatus tendonitis. The production of symptoms in the painful arc. Pain is felt on abduction as the inflamed tendon moves beneath the acromion.

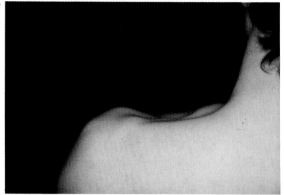

180 Bicipital tendonitis. A clinical photograph showing localized swelling over the anterior aspect of the shoulder due to inflammation and effusion into the biceps tendon sheath.

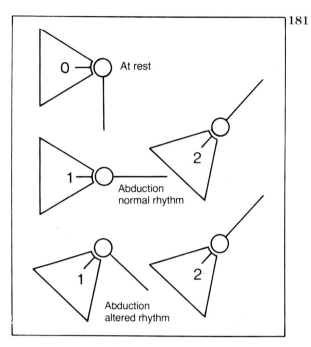

181 Scapulohumeral rhythm. The normal pattern with initial abduction at shoulder joint and the altered rhythm with abduction by rotation of scapula.

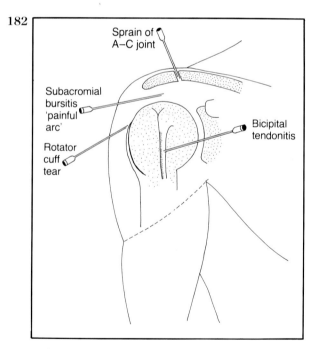

182 Sites of injection for common causes of shoulder pain.

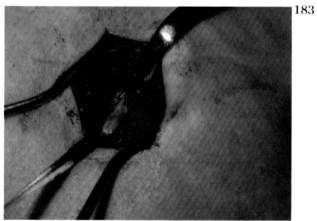

183 Thickened tendon sheath displayed at decompression of the long head of biceps for recalcitrant bicipital tendovaginitis.

The management of shoulder injuries in sportsmen is similar to that for the population as a whole. Diffuse lesions such as capsulitis are best treated with systemic anti-inflammatory medication and physiotherapy (eg, shortwave diathermy), while well-localized lesions usually respond well to local anaesthetic and steroid injection.

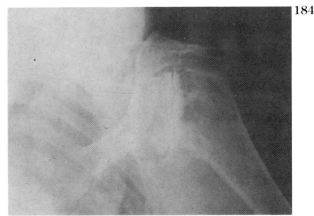

184

184 Degenerative disease – osteoarthrosis of the shoulder joint. A rare condition often associated with a history of recurrent dislocation.

Dislocation and subluxation

185

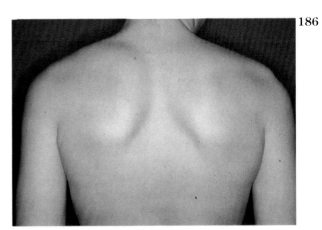

186

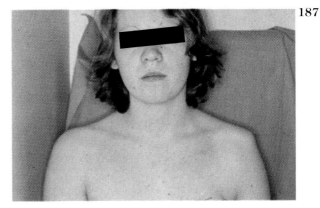

187

185 The common mechanism of dislocation. The arm is forcibly abducted and externally rotated, either in a fall or in a pile-up, as in this ice hockey incident, giving anterior dislocation.

186 Subluxation – right shoulder. This may recur and be regularly reproduced as a 'habit spasm'.

187 Dislocation (anterior) – clinical appearance of the most common type.

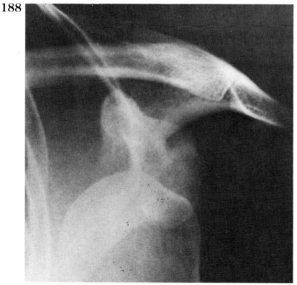

188 An anterior dislocation – X-ray appearance.

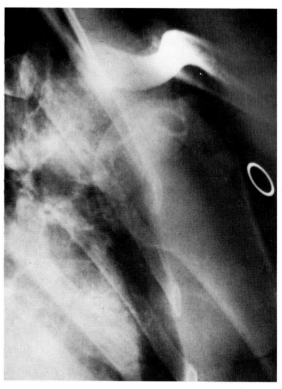

189 A posterior dislocation – X-ray appearance. This is much less common than an anterior dislocation.

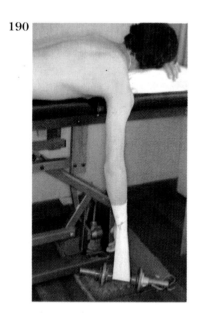

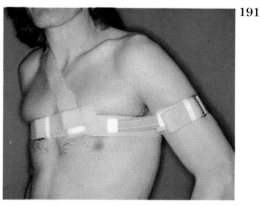

191 **Check rein** to allow movement of the shoulder (without abduction) during rehabilitation. Jockeys often return to the saddle early wearing such a device.

190 **Reduction of dislocation by Stimson method.** This is gentle manipulation and can be carried out immediately after dislocation. Note that the weight (in this case a dumbell) *hangs* on the arm and is not held by the patient. Reduction takes place with time as the patient relaxes.

Injuries of the upper arm

Injuries of the upper arm are relatively unusual although a few examples are well known. They differ little from similar injuries sustained in non-sporting activity.

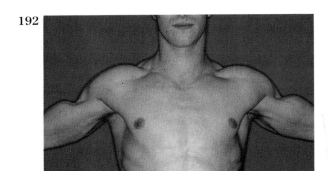

192 Bilateral rupture of the long head of the biceps brachii. In this particular case, the victim – a gymnast – felt both tendons snap one after the other while exercising on the rings.

193 Defective biceps. The same gymnast competing internationally after subsequent rehabilitation. The defect in the biceps is clearly seen, but is of little functional significance.

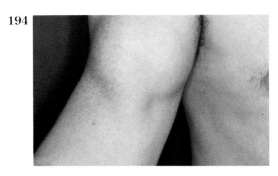

194 Rupture of the biceps tendon itself is less common than rupture of the tendon of the long head of the biceps.

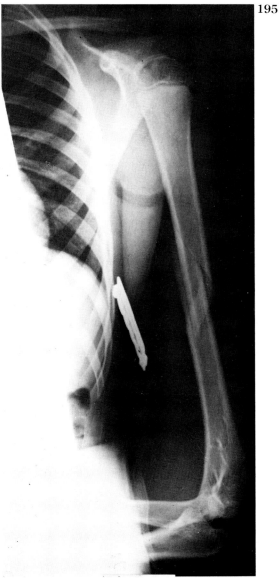

195 Gymnastic injury. Spiral fracture of the humerus as a result of a fall from apparatus. Note that in this type of fracture radial nerve involvement is common, with wrist-drop and extensor weakness.

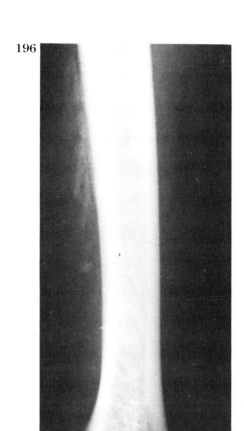

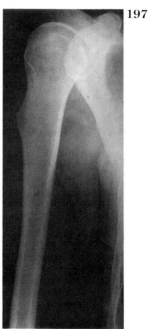

197 Benign exostosis – a red herring which presented in a patient with overlying referred pain from the cervical spine.

196 Myositis ossificans. An X-ray showing ectopic bone deposit in the brachialis on the anterior aspect of the humerus. This was reabsorbed in six months.

Epiphysitis may occur at either end of the humerus in 'little league' and 'pitcher's arm' – these are overuse injuries which recover well with rest, provided the patient is not forced to play too soon after the symptoms subside.

In some cases muscular violence may of itself be sufficient to cause a fracture of the humerus, and spontaneous fracture has been described in a number of throwing accidents. It seems to be most common in baseball.

7 Elbow injuries

Congenital abnormalities

Mechanical abnormalities may interfere with sport.

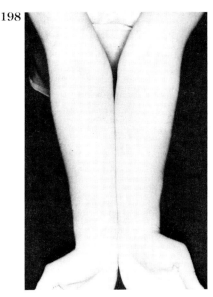

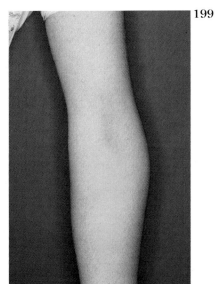

198 Cubitus valgus. This deformity predisposes to ulnar neuritis, particularly in throwers.

199 Cubitus varus. This may be the result of an earlier supracondylar fracture. The joint is vulnerable in racquet games.

200 Cubitus recurvatus – often a feature of hypermobile joint disease. This predisposes the sufferer to olecranon impingement exostosis.

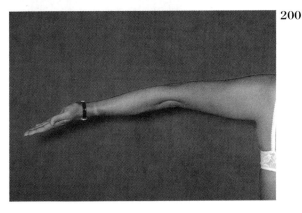

Structural abnormalities of the elbow are commonly congenital although they may be acquired, usually as a result of a childhood elbow fracture affecting the epiphyses, which subsequently disturbs the normal growth of the lower end of the humerus. Cubitus valgus, varus and recurvatus may all cause problems, typically in sports involving throwing. Cubitus recurvatus may also cause problems in gymnastics.

Fractures and dislocations

Fractures about the elbow, as well as dislocations, require serious attention. Inadequate management, particularly in the early stages, may lead to permanent disability with disfigurement and loss of joint mobility. In dislocations and some fractures, particularly in children, the possibility of associated vascular and nerve damage must be remembered.

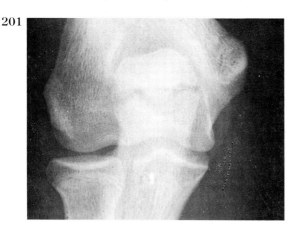

201 Fracture of the olecranon – often due to indirect violence, ie violent contraction of the triceps brachiae.

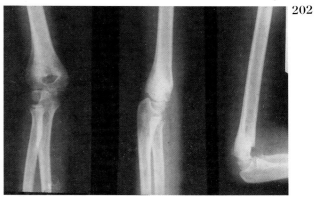

202 Displaced lower humeral epiphysis (supracondylar fracture) following a fall from gymnastic apparatus.

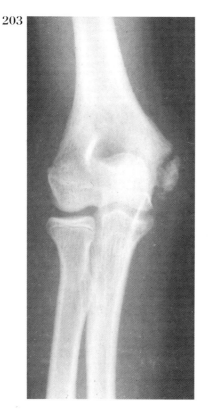

203 Avulsion of medial epicondyle – X-ray appearance. This type of injury is the result of indirect violence. The common flexor origin was pulled away in a gymnastic accident.

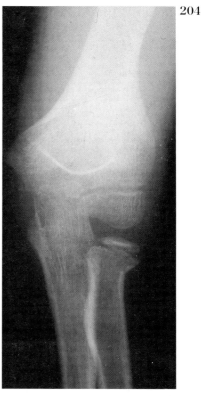

204 Greenstick fracture of the neck of the radius due to a fall on the outstretched hand.

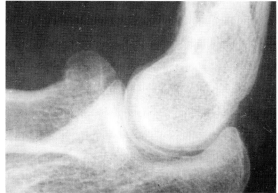

205 Fracture of the radial head. This also resulted from a fall on the outstretched hand. If a fragment is displaced some functional loss may follow.

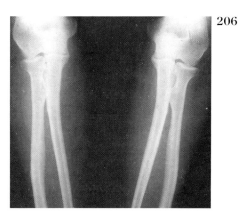

206 Distortion of left radial head such as may follow a displaced fracture. This may interfere with pronation and supination of the forearm.

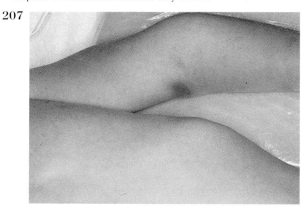

207 Dislocation of elbow – clinical appearance. This is usually the result of severe violence such as a fall from gymnastic apparatus.

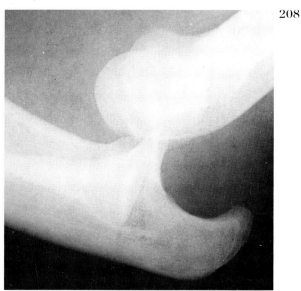

208 Dislocation of elbow joint – X-ray appearance.

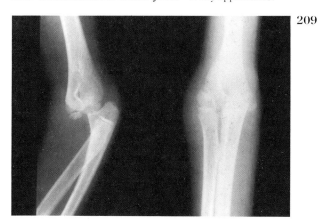

209 Elbow dislocation in a child – note the associated epiphyseal damage.

The effects of mismanagement of fractures about the elbow, particularly in children, may be disastrous.

210 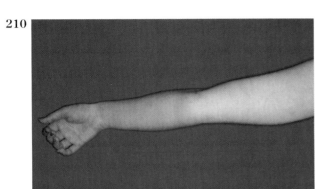 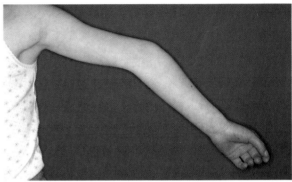 211

210 and **211** Deformity of the left elbow in a young gymnast due to mismanagement of a fracture dislocation of the upper end of the radius. Normal (**210**) and deformed (**211**) elbow.

212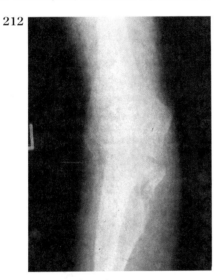

212 X-ray appearance of dislocation in 211. Note dislocated radial head and ectopic calcification.

213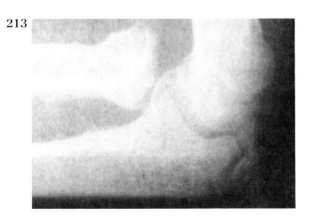

213 Mismanaged dislocation of the radial head – another case of mismanagement in a gymnast.

Osteochondritis

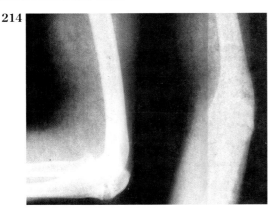

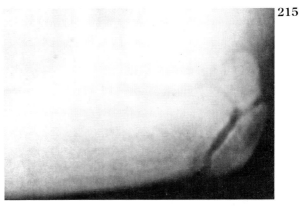

214 Olecranon fracture – avulsion type. Note the fracture line more distal on the olecranon than the epiphyseal line.

215 Osteochondritis of olecranon epiphysis in a male tennis player (aged 14) – X-ray appearance. It is not clear whether this is a true traction epiphysitis caused by the pull on the triceps tendon, or whether there is an element of impingement injury resulting from repeated forced extension of the elbow joint. As with Sever's disease (q.v.), the X-ray appearance may be misleading and the diagnosis is essentially clinical and by bone scan.

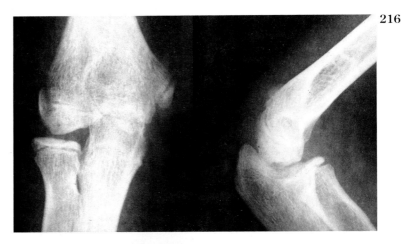

216 Osteochondritis of the trochlea in a female gymnast (aged 12) with loose body formation.

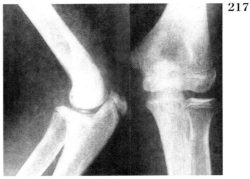

217 Osteochondritis of the capitellum in a young judoka showing loose body formation.

These cases illustrate the damage that can accrue to the joints of highly talented young sportsmen and women who are overstrained in training during their formative years.

Ectopic calcification

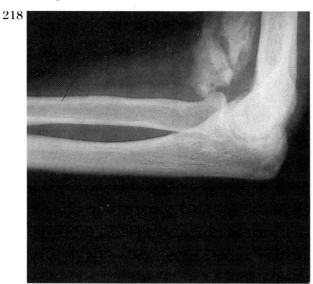

218 Ectopic calcification in capsule after major joint trauma.

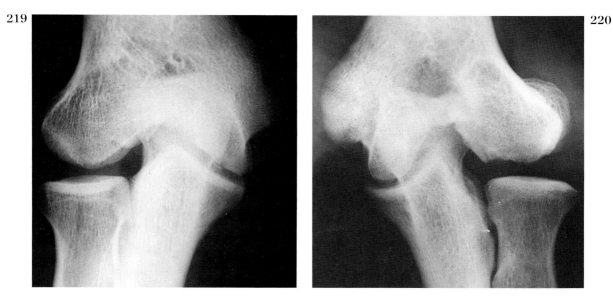

219 and **220 Limited extension.** X-rays of the elbow joints in a young rugby player with limited extension. Probably congenital, as the other elbow was identical.

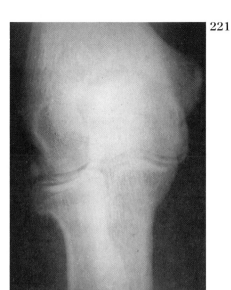

221

221 Synovial diverticulum outlined in an arthrogram. This caused a locking of the elbow due to the pannus acting as a radiolucent loose body.

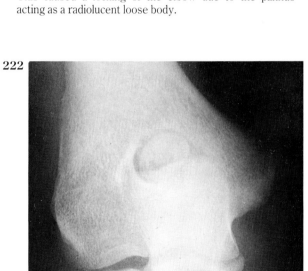

222

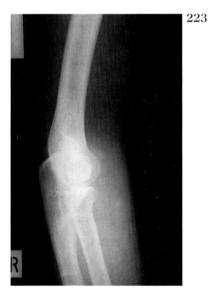

223

222 Olecranon fossa abnormality. This congenital abnormality in the olecranon fossa of a cricketer (fast bowler) meant he was unable to extend his elbow fully, which in turn led to his being no-balled frequently (for chucking) when bowling.

223 Lateral X-ray of 222.

Loose bodies – elbow

Loose bodies in the elbow, as elsewhere, may cause pain and discomfort related to their predisposing pathology and will also produce locking by interference with normal joint mechanism. In the latter case surgical removal is necessary but the long-term outcome is not necessarily good.

224 Handball is a sport demanding a vigorous forward extension of the elbow.

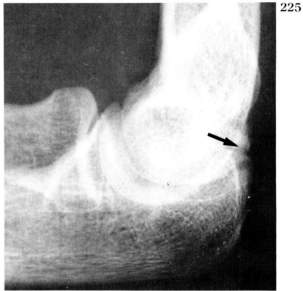

225 Loose bodies due to separation of impingement exostosis on the tip of the olecranon process of the ulna, in an international handball player.

The exostosis develops as a result of repeated banging of the tip of the olecranon into its fossa during forced hyperextension.

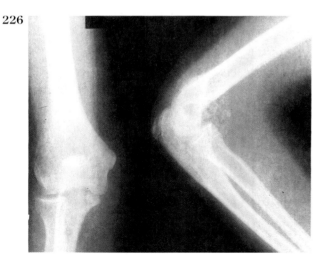

226 Loose body in elbow secondary to osteochondritis dissecans in a gymnast.

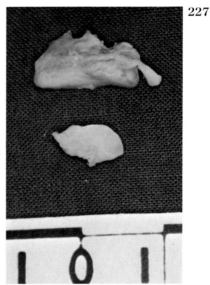

227 Specimen of loose body after surgical removal.

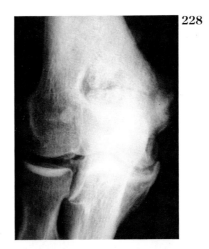

228 Loose bodies associated with degenerative joint disease in a squash player. This condition is seen in baseball players and is known as 'pitcher's elbow'.

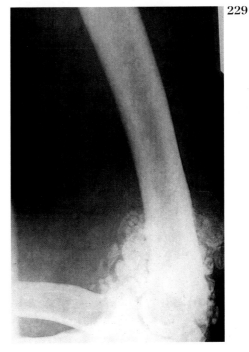

229

229 Multiple calcifying loose bodies in synovial chondromatosis.

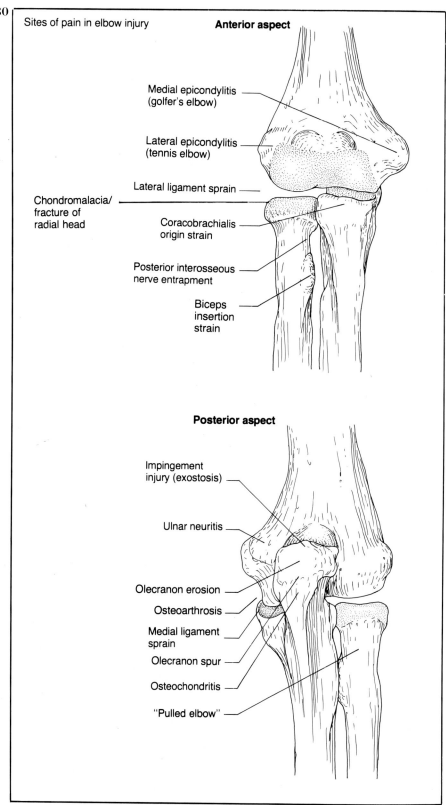

230

Sites of pain in elbow injury

Anterior aspect

Medial epicondylitis
(golfer's elbow)

Lateral epicondylitis
(tennis elbow)

Lateral ligament sprain

Chondromalacia/
fracture of
radial head

Coracobrachialis
origin strain

Posterior interosseous
nerve entrapment

Biceps
insertion
strain

Posterior aspect

Impingement
injury (exostosis)

Ulnar neuritis

Olecranon erosion

Osteoarthrosis

Medial ligament
sprain

Olecranon spur

Osteochondritis

"Pulled elbow"

230 Sites of pain – differential diagnosis of elbow pain.

Lateral epicondylitis (tennis elbow)

Common causes of this condition include playing a whipped (topspin) backhand at tennis and using a badminton racket with too small a handle.

231 Topspin backhand. Note the position of the racket head in the application of heavy topspin.

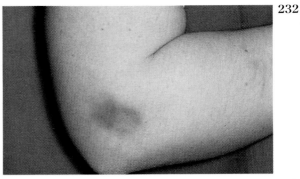

232 Lateral epicondylitis. Marked bruising over the lateral epicondyle in a recent case of acute tennis elbow.

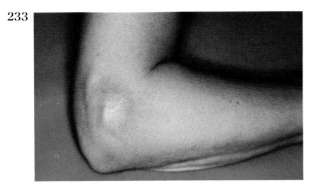

233 Skin change over lateral epicondyle as a result of a previous hydrocortisone injection. Note the discoloration of the skin – this is associated with a thinning of the dermis and a loss of subcutaneous fat.

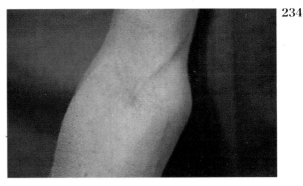

234 Cystic change in the common extensor origin producing a marked swelling over the lateral epicondyle.

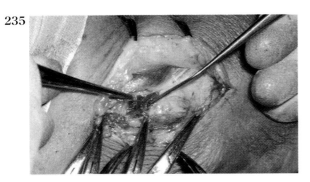

235 Surgical tenotomy of common extensor origin for tennis elbow. A radical method of treatment for recalcitrant chronic lesions.

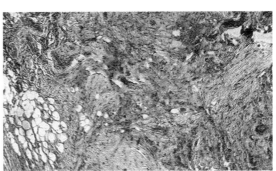

236 Scar tissue – histological appearance. Scar tissue removed at tenotomy, showing a completely random mixture of old and new scar tissue formation.

Golfer's elbow

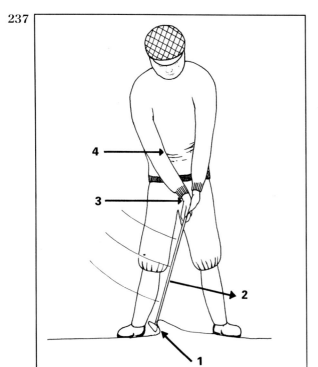

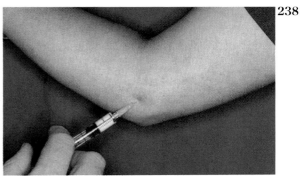

238 Medial epicondylitis. Golfer's elbow treated by local anaesthetic and steroid injection into the tender muscle attachment.

237 Common flexor origin. Club head blocked (**1**) causes forward rotation of shaft (**2**), forcibly hyperextending wrist (**3**), and pulling common flexor origin (**4**).

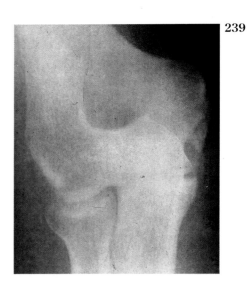

239 Calcification in common flexor mass – X-ray appearance. This is a late complication of recurrent golfer's elbow.

Thrower's elbow (medial collateral ligament sprain)

240 Mechanism of injury – the 'round arm' throw.

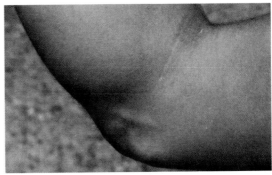

241 Clinical appearance with loss of normal common flexor muscle bulk.

This condition should not be treated with local anaesthetic and steroid injection in view of the risk of subsequent laxity or rupture – an all-too-common complication at this site.

Pulled elbow

Subluxation of the radial head in children. This is a condition in which the head of the radius is pulled out of the annular ligament as a result of traction on the arm. It occurs in body-contact sports including judo. Associated fractures are uncommon and usually self-evident.

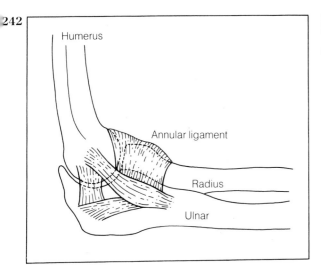

242 Normal anatomy of annular ligament and pulled elbow.

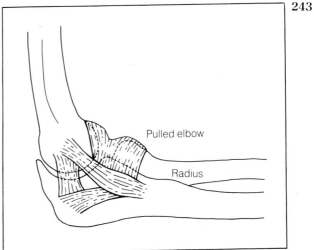

243 Mechanism of pulled elbow.

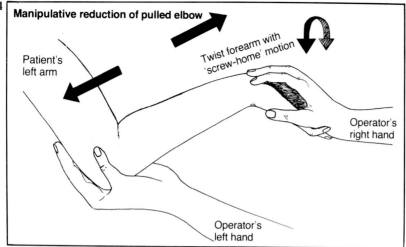

244 Manipulative reduction of pulled elbow

Patient's left arm

Twist forearm with 'screw-home' motion

Operator's right hand

Operator's left hand

244 Manipulation. Reduce with the elbow at a right angle by a rotary screwing movement of alternate pronation and supination of forearm while pushing the radius towards the elbow. Reduction is easily achieved, accompanied by a palpable click.

Elbow joint – degenerative changes

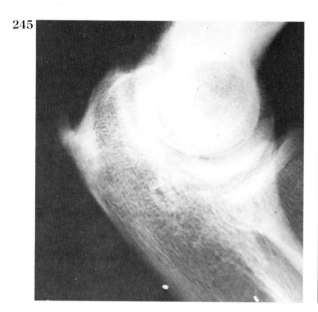

245 Spur on the tip of the olecranon at triceps insertion in a tennis player.

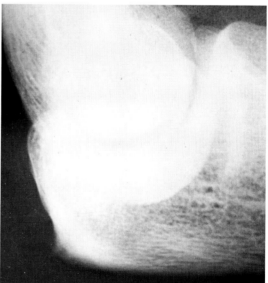

246 Erosion on the tip of the olecranon at triceps insertion in an international fencer.

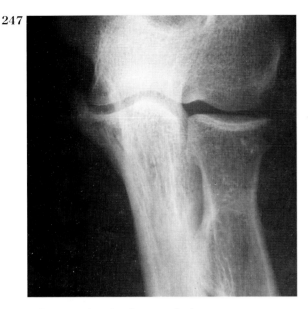

247 Spur on the ulna in a squash player.

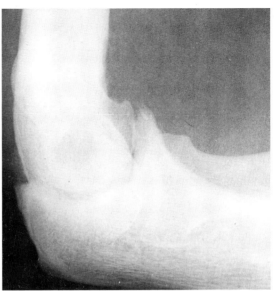

248 Spur on the coronoid process in a badminton player.

These lesions may be left undisturbed unless they are causing localized symptoms. Then, conservative treatment (eg, local anaesthetic and steroid injection) may be inadequate – particularly if there is any mechanical disturbance – in which case surgical removal may be necessary.

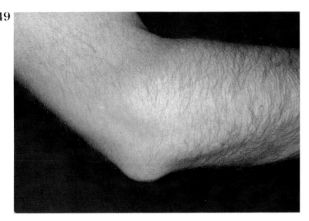

249 Olecranon bursa yields to short-wave diathermy. Aspiration is not indicated as it induces loculation and fibrosis.

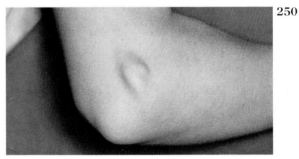

250 Ganglion over the lateral epicondyle – something of a rarity.

8 Forearm, wrist and hand injuries

Tenosynovitis of the extensor tendons of the wrist

251 and **252 Tenosynovitis.** This condition is common in oarsmen and canoeists, and is often associated with training in rough water.

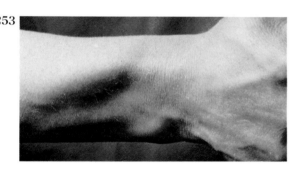

253 Tenosynovitis. Swelling and crepitus on the dorsum of the forearm.

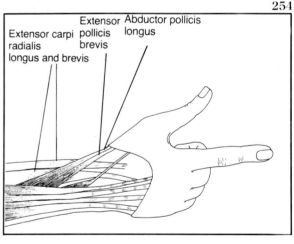

254 Anatomy of the abductor pollicis longus and the extensor pollicis brevis overlying the radial extensors of the wrist. The muscle bellies are frequently hypertrophied and oedematous in this condition with adhesion to the underlying tissues

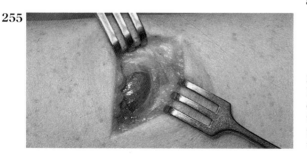

255 Surgical decompression of abductor pollicis longus and extensor pollicis brevis muscles gives early and effective relief, as the muscle bulges up through the incision in the sheath, relieving pressure on the tendons beneath. Return to normal function is possible within a matter of hours.

Congenital abnormalities

Congenital abnormalities may present as injuries in sport through interference with wrist function.

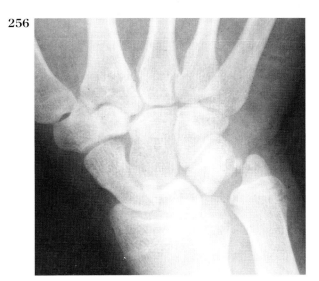

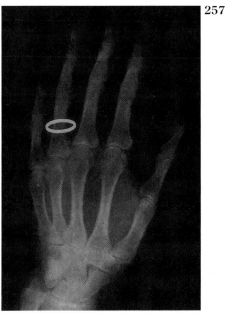

256 Prominence of the ulnar styloid associated with a chip fracture. This patient complained of inability to push the hand into ulnar deviation together with pain while playing racket games.

257 Congenital fusion of trapezius and trapezoid impairing thumb function.

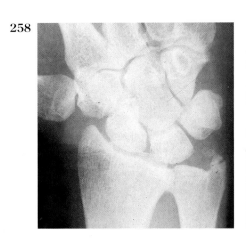

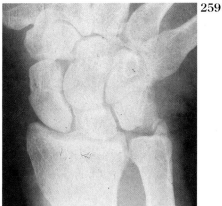

258 and **259 Radiographs of the wrist in radial (258) and ulnar (deviation)** readily demonstrate impingement of the carpus on the ulnar styloid in the latter.

Wrist injuries

Wrist injuries are relatively uncommon, but may be a source of considerable disability. Fractures and sprains are no different from those incurred in normal activities, but impingement lesions, as for example in 'thrower's wrist', are not commonly met outside sport.

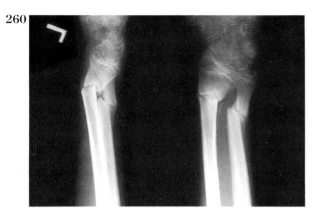

260 Greenstick fracture of the lower radius and ulna – a judo injury in an adolescent.

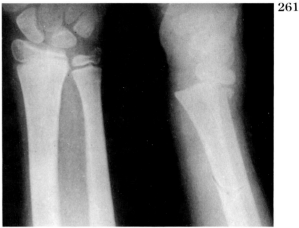

261 Epiphysiolysis with displacement in a soccer player.

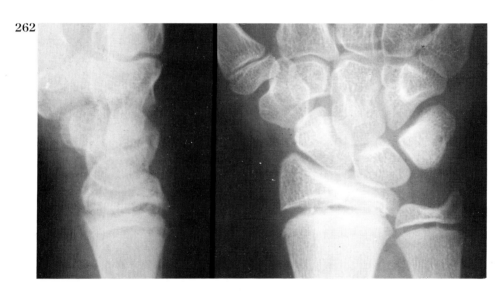

262 Epiphysiolysis without displacement in a young gymnast. Note the appearance of the epiphyseal line. This condition should be treated as a fracture and immobilized.

Radio-ulnar joint injury

Injury to the distal radio-ulnar joint is an occasional source of disability. Interference with pronation and supination may be due to loose body or dislocation of the triangular meniscus and will often require surgical exploration.

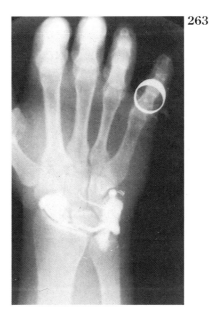

263 Rupture of the triangular cartilage. Arthrogram showing dye leaking into the proximal synovial pouch of the inferior radio-ulnar joint.

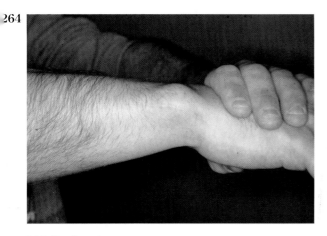

264 Radio-ulnar subluxation. Inferior radio-ulnar subluxation after a fall from a horse.

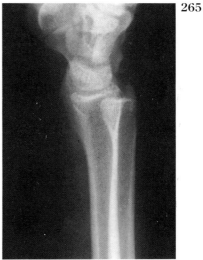

265 X-ray of 264.

Radiocarpal joint injury

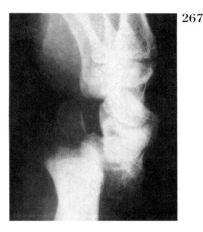

266 Dislocation of the lunate.

267 X-ray of perilunar fracture dislocation of the wrist – a rare injury, in this case due to a fall during a rugby match. It may cause severe median nerve compression.

Carpal injuries

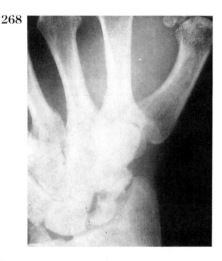

268 X-ray of an ununited fracture of the scaphoid. This injury commonly occurs in a fall on an outstretched hand and may be undetected in the early stages. Early diagnosis and effective immobilization obviate the risk of non-union and later osteoarthrosis.

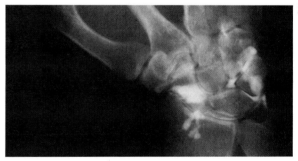

269 Carpal subluxation. Note the misalignment of the lunate and triquetral in this arthrogram of a tennis player with a painful wrist.

In some cases of persistent wrist pain associated with an apparent chronic sprain, stress X-rays in radial and ulnar deviation may demonstrate traumatic diastasis of the scaphoid from the lunate.

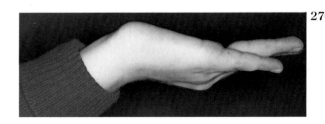

270 Chondromalacia of the pisiform – swelling on the pisiform in a polo player.

Hand and wrist injuries

271 'Thrower's wrist'–hyperextension. Putting the shot. Note marked hyperextension of the wrist as the athlete accelerates the shot in the action of projecting it.

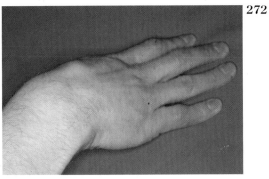

272 A prominent Lister's tubercle (2nd metatarsal styloid process). It sometimes causes impingement lesions, ie thrower's wrist.

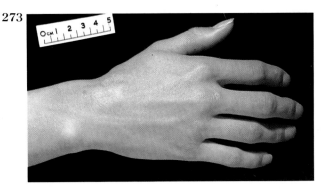

273 Extensor tenosynovitis – this may be confused with thrower's wrist but pain and tenderness are more diffuse and not restricted to extreme hyperextension. In this case note the steroid stigmata due to previous injections.

274 A ganglion. Soft tissue swelling on the dorsum of the wrist, a common problem.

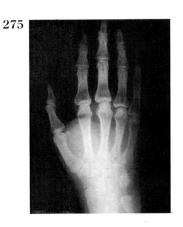

275 Acute infective tenosynovitis of the extensor tendons – note the carpal decalcification due to hyperaemia shown in this X-ray.

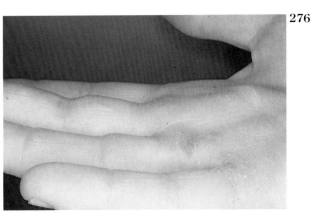

276 Trigger finger in a fencer. The nodule in the flexor tendon is clearly seen.

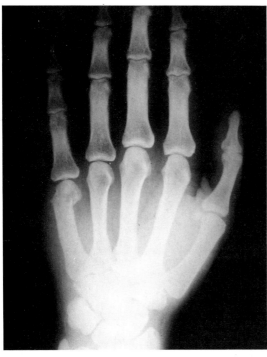

277 Metacarpal fracture. These are often self-inflicted when the patient engages in foul play in body-contact sport and punches an opponent.

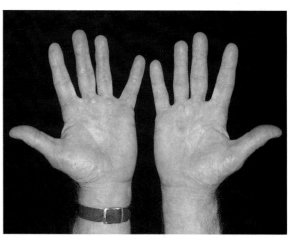

278 Median nerve palsy in a handball player – note thenar wasting.

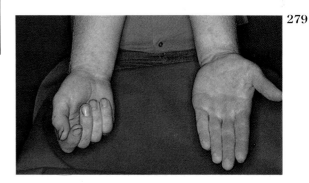

279 Interosseous nerve palsy – a real oddity. Anterior interosseous nerve palsy in a tyro-water skier from a traction injury.

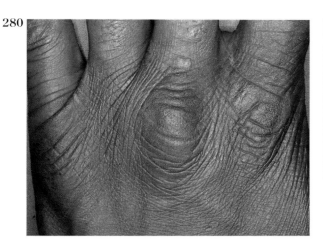

280 'Boxer's knuckle'. Adventitious bursa on (3rd) metacarpal head.

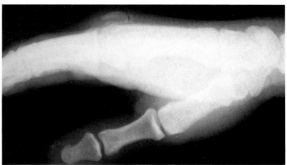

281 'Bursagram' – an X-ray of an adventitious bursa in boxer's knuckle.

Thumb injuries

Thumb injuries are common in boxing, and in other circumstances in which a punch is badly thrown.

Boxing gloves often hold the fist open and fail to protect.

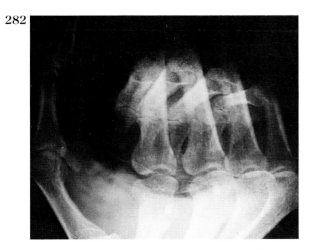

282 X-ray of a fist clenched within boxing glove showing vulnerability of thumb.

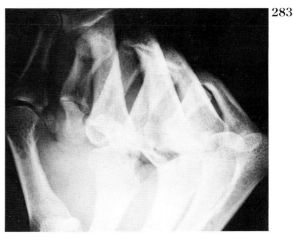

283 Ungloved fist for comparison.

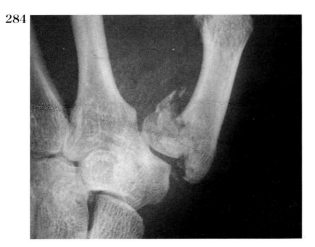

284 Bennett's fracture. Fracture of the base of the 1st metacarpal through the joint line.

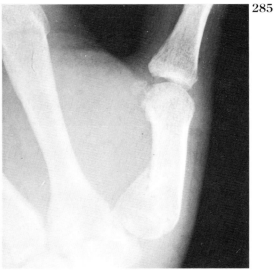

285 Fracture of the base of the 1st metacarpal with no joint involvement.

286

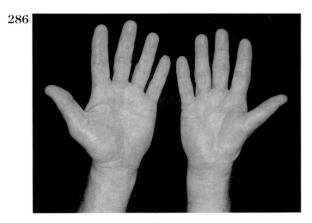

286 Rupture of the ulnar collateral ligament of the thumb.

287

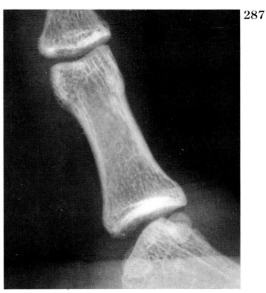

287 Dislocation of the thumb associated with rupture of the ulnar collateral ligament in an Olympic medallist (otherwise known as 'gamekeeper's thumb').

288

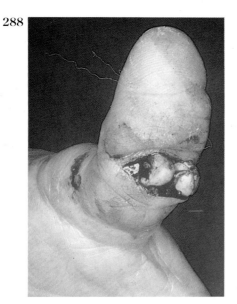

288 Compound dislocation of the thumb. For a change, a rugby injury!

289

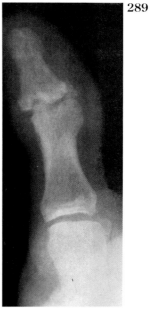

289 Terminal phalangeal fracture at the interphalangeal joint due to an end-on blow in basketball.

Finger injuries

These injuries are common in body-contact sports, hard ball games (especially cricket and baseball), and in judo (which involves grasping the opponent's clothing).

290

290 Fingers are at risk in any catching game, but particularly in cricket.

291

291 Some protection is obtained by wearing suitably padded gloves – like the baseball catcher's.

292

292 Finger damage in judo occurs when a hold on the opponent's clothing is forcibly broken.

Phalangeal fractures

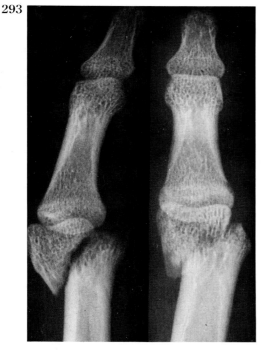

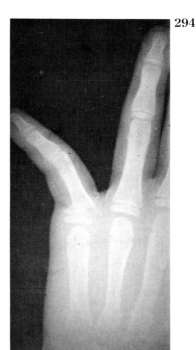

293 Proximal phalangeal fracture can occur when the hand grasping an implement, eg a hockey stick, is struck directly by a hard ball.

294 Fracture at the base of the proximal phalanx due to abduction injury in a fall on a dry ski slope.

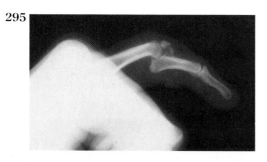

295 Fracture dislocation of proximal interphalangeal joint – a rugby injury.

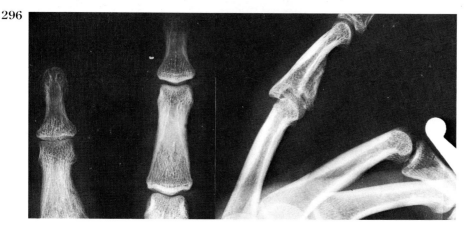

296 Fracture of the middle phalanx is relatively uncommon and, like that of the proximal, often caused by a blow from a ball, in this case from a cricket ball.

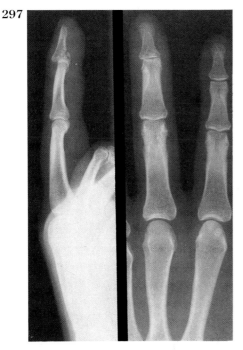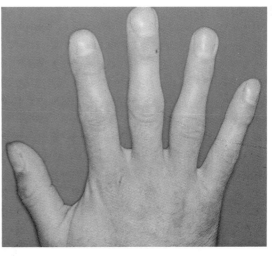

297

298

297 Terminal phalangeal fractures are very common not only in hard-ball games but also in basketball, volleyball and handball. In some cases, particularly with a direct blow in the long axis of the phalanx, the fracture line goes through the bone with disruption of the distal interphalangeal joint.

298 Other common finger injuries include interphalangeal subluxation or dislocation. Residual swelling and some stiffness is not uncommon but can be minimized by active rehabilitation. The photograph shows an old dislocation, the result of repeated injury in a judoka. Functional deformity is always preferable to loss of function, irrespective of cosmetic appearances.

Tendon injury

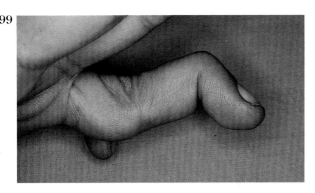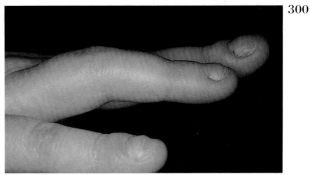

299

300

299 Mallet finger. Rupture of the extensor tendon or avulsion of attachment due to a blow on the tip of the finger, as can occur whilst slip fielding in cricket.

300 Boutonnière deformity with rupture of the extensor hood over the proximal interphalangeal joint.

Other conditions

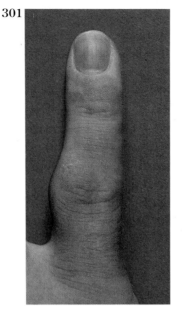

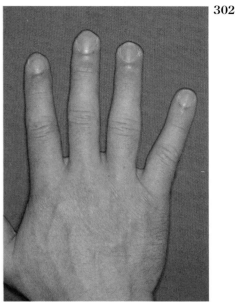

301 Tender callosity on the proximal interphalangeal joint of the right little finger of a golfer using the interlocking grip.

302 Ten-pin bowler's fingers – swelling over the proximal interphalangeal joints due to finger pressure in holes of a ten-pin bowl.

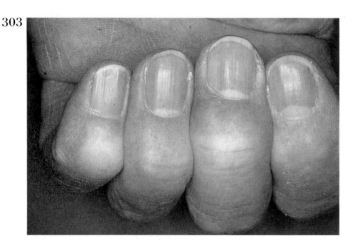

303 Ganglion over distal interphalangeal joints in a golfer with degenerative joint disease – these are cystic and translucent, unlike Heberden's nodes.

9 Trunk and abdominal injuries

Trunk injury

Most trunk injuries involve the musculoskeletal system of the spine and limb roots. Thoracic cage injuries are also quite common, and the ever-present possibility of rib fracture associated with underlying visceral damage must be borne in mind.

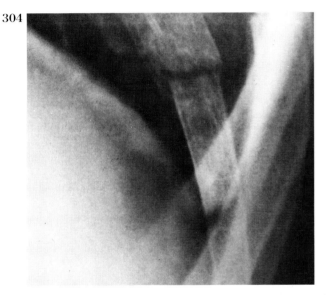

304 Rib fractures are common in rugby and riding accidents, but may also occur as the result of a direct blow in any sport.

There is a tendency not to strap or support these injuries to avoid reducing respiratory excursion. However, patients will breathe more easily and deeply with suitable strapping – pain is a more potent inhibitor of adequate ventilation.

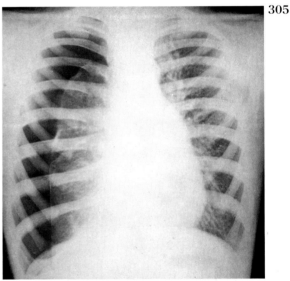

305 Pneumothorax associated with rib fracture – X-ray appearance.

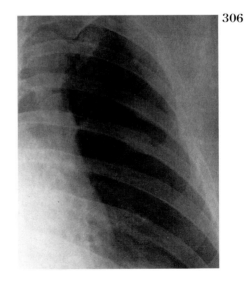

306 Stress fracture of the angle of the rib due to repeated muscular exertion, serving at tennis,

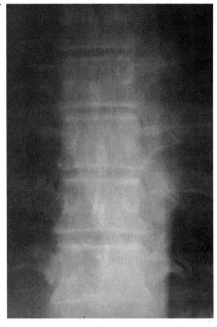

307 Costo-vertebral osteoarthrosis – a cause of pain in the mid back in a golfer.

Other problems of trunk pathology may affect sports participation because they cause concern on the part of the patient rather than because of any immediate clinical reason. Congenital abnormalities may look disfiguring but are usually of little functional significance.

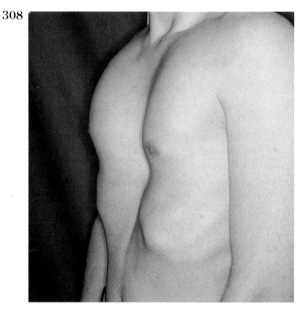

308 Pectus excavatus – a congenital abnormality of the chest. The patient was able to resume vigorous sporting activity after surgery to restore the normal contour of the sternum.

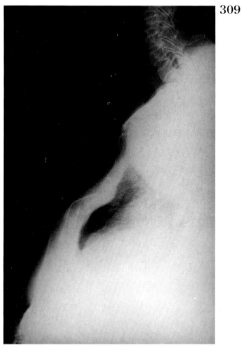

309 Sternal fracture. A less common injury, usually the sequel of a vehicular injury.

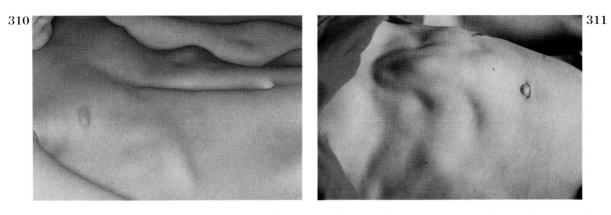

310 and **311 Defects in the linea alba** – congenital abnormalities seen in two young soccer players. A matter of academic rather than clinical importance!

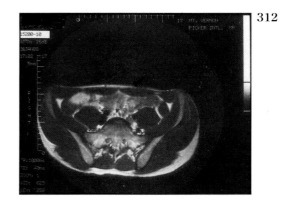

312 Rectus abdominis muscle tear demonstrated on an MRI scan.

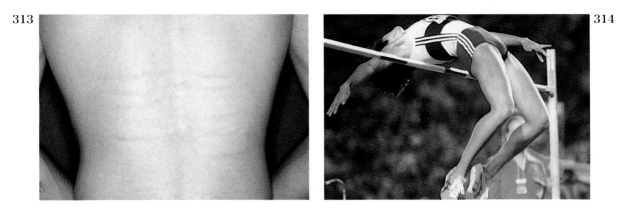

313 and **314 Weals** on the back of an athlete. The patient was a high jumper practising the Fosbury flop, repeatedly falling onto the landing area with the bar beneath him.

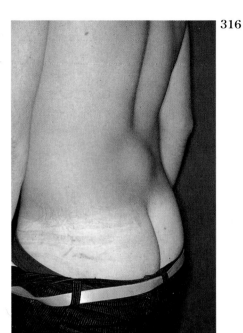

315 Intramuscular lipoma in the serratus anterior – an unusual embarrassment for a sportsman.

316 Benign subcutaneous lipoma (but smaller swellings in this area may be associated with spina bifida).

Abdominal injury

Soft tissue injury to the abdominal and pelvic viscera is rare in sport. When it does occur, it is often associated with high velocity impact accidents – and occasionally with deliberate violence.

317 Water can be very unyielding – abdominal injury occurs in high velocity impacts.

318 Direct violence may also cause abdominal injury.

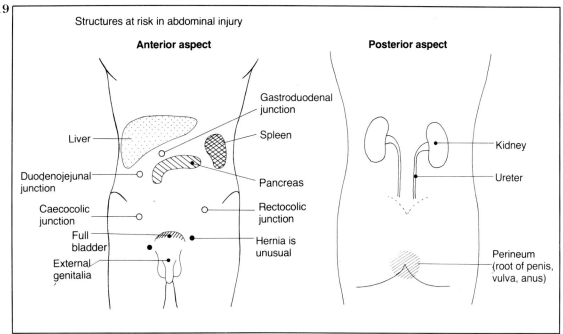

319

Structures at risk in abdominal injury

Anterior aspect

Posterior aspect

Liver

Gastroduodenal junction

Spleen

Duodenojejunal junction

Pancreas

Caecocolic junction

Rectocolic junction

Full bladder

Hernia is unusual

External genitalia

Kidney

Ureter

Perineum (root of penis, vulva, anus)

319 Sites at risk in direct abdominal injury.

In the abdomen the structures at risk include liver, spleen and pancreas, together with the bowel, particularly when it becomes retroperitoneal. Thus the gastroduodenal and duodenojejunal junctions are particularly at risk. The large bowel is much more rarely involved in accidents of this type but it may be involved in penetrating injuries.

The genitourinary tract is also vulnerable, the kidneys to a blow in the loin, and the bladder (particularly if full) and urethra to a blow in the lower abdomen and perineum.

An interesting form of orchitis has been described in youngsters going for early morning runs before emptying their bladders. Male external genitalia should always be protected at least by a supporter or jockey briefs and in hard-ball games such as cricket and hockey by a properly constructed box manufactured to BS 6183 (in Britain) or an equivalent standard.

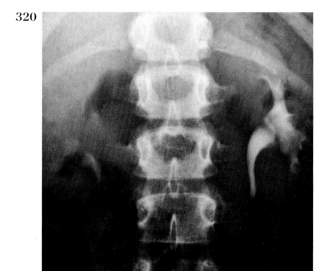

320

320 Intravenous pyelogram showing damage to right kidney.

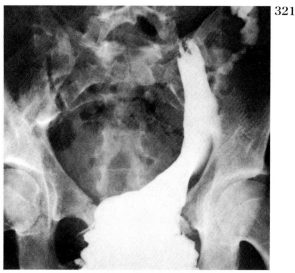

321

321 Cystogram showing extravasation of blood caused by rupture of the bladder.

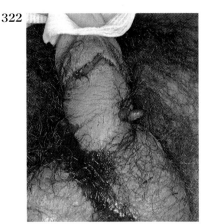

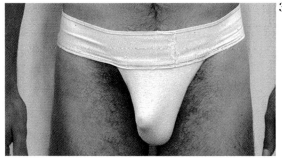

322 Genital injuries also occur in sport. Lacerations of the penis from a direct kick in a soccer accident.

323 Wearing an athletic supporter or jock-strap reduces the risk of injury.

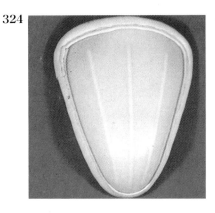

324 Protective gear – the box often worn by hockey players and virtually all cricketers. Not only should batsmen wear one, but also close fielders – especially those in the 'silly' positions.

325 Water-skiing accident. In such instances water under pressure may be forced into the vagina (and even into the rectum) if adequate protective clothing is not worn.

The female genitalia are less vulnerable, as might be expected, but water-skiing presents particular problems of high pressure douche from an awkward fall. Adequate protection must be worn for serious competition and training.

Injury to the external genitalia of female children requires particular care in management due to the possibility that it may be an indication of child sexual abuse.

Acquired hernia or rupture is unusual in sportsmen, probably because the well-developed abdominal muscles in the sportsman protect vulnerable sites. Incipient hernia may be a cause of groin pain, however, and needs to be differentiated from traumatic osteitis pubis (**391** and **392**).

Injuries to the abdominal wall are relatively uncommon and typically involve contusions from direct blows and muscle tears from intrinsic violence.

In all cases of abdominal injury the risk of visceral damage must be kept in mind, particularly if any form of direct violence is involved. Patients should be kept under strict observation and admitted to hospital if there is any deterioration in their condition. The ever-present risk of misdiagnosing the silent abdomen should be remembered and the patient must be observed at repeated intervals after a direct blow on the abdomen before he can be regarded as being safe.

Spontaneous bleeding either as haematuria or as haemoglobinuria is an occasional feature in high performance sport. The exact cause is uncertain. In some instances it results from damage to the red corpuscles in the active tissues. in others it is due to altered glomerular filtration dynamics and some instances of haematuria may be caused by trigonitis. The presence of blood in the urine should always be investigated; and as a matter of urgency if this symptom is associated with direct trauma.

10 Spinal injuries

Dorsal spine

Being well buttressed by the ribs, the spine is not greatly troubled by injury – except in the case of severe riding and vehicular accidents, in which very heavy loads, often with a rotary component, are applied. Fractures tend to occur at the upper or lower end of thè dorsal spine. The spinous processes give more protection from D 4 to D 8.

Soft tissue injuries are quite common, as are intervertebral joint conditions – including the 'locked facet' syndrome and the 'dorsal disc' syndrome with referred pain along an intercostal nerve. Osteochondritis (adolescent kyphosis) quite commonly interferes with sport.

326 High speed vehicular accidents are a common cause of spinal injury.

327 Injury to the dorsal spine is typically the result of a combination of flexion compression and rotation stress.

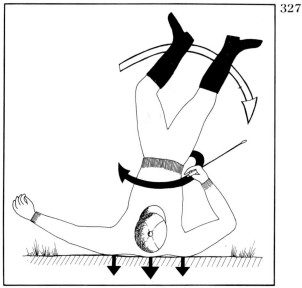

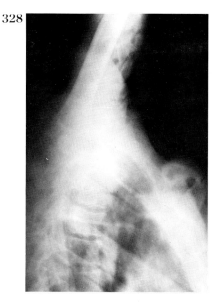

328 Upper dorsal spinal fracture.

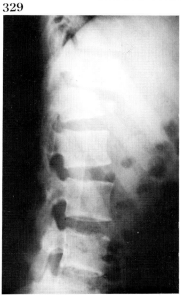

329 Lower dorsal spinal fracture.

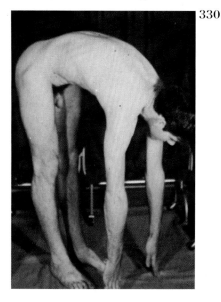

330 Osteochondritis (adolescent kyphosis) – loss of normal spinal contour.

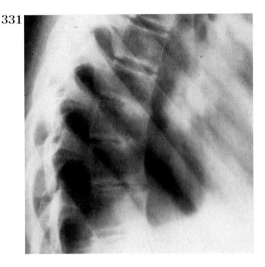

331 Congenitally fused dorsal vertebrae. This condition may cause pain in patients needing a high level of flexibility, eg gymnasts (see also cervical and lumbar congenital anomalies).

Lumbar spine: congenital abnormality

These congenital abnormalities are a source of weakness in the spine which may be productive of symptoms in a patient undergoing heavy weight training and exercise programmes. The problem is essentially mechanical, usually associated with distortion of the intervertebral joint surfaces. These are generally a contraindication to such activities as weight lifting, rowing and athletic throwing events.

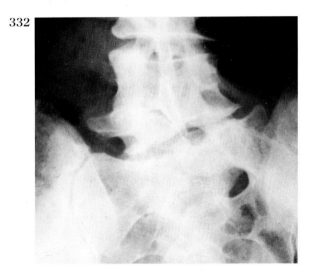

332 Hemivertebra – an anteroposterior X-ray.

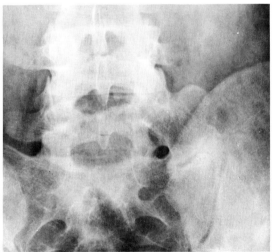

333 Sacralization – an anteroposterior X-ray showing partial sacralization (left side) of the 5th lumbar vertebra.

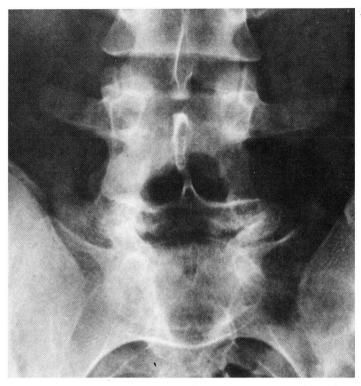

334

334 Partial lumbarization of the 1st sacral vertebra – an anteroposterior X-ray.

In these conditions spinal stresses are transmitted asymmetrically and so introduce abnormal torque effects.

335

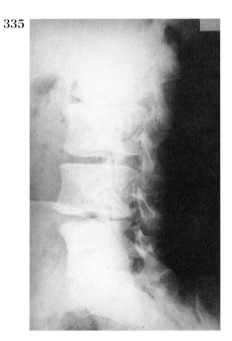

336

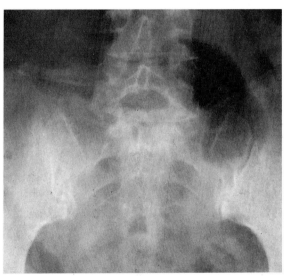

336 Congenitally long 5th lumbar transverse process.

335 Spondylolysis in a congenitally abnormal lumbar vertebra.

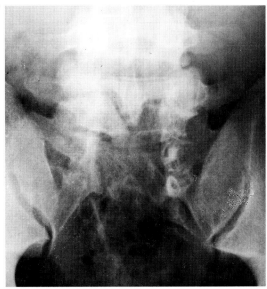

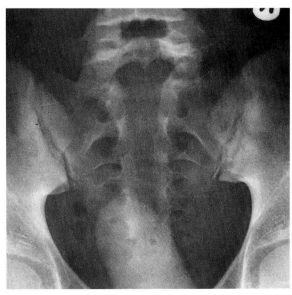

337 Spina bifida occulta with distortion of the posterior facetal joints – an anteroposterior X-ray.

338 Spina bifida occulta – a more severe case – which did not prevent active participation at senior level by an oarsman.

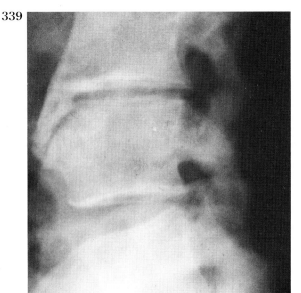

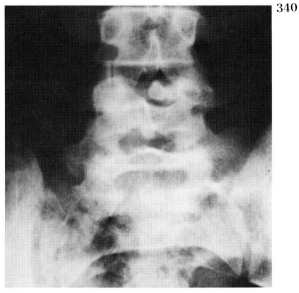

339 Lumbar vertebra – abnormal ossification limbus vertebra.

340 Congenital abnormalities – an anteroposterior X-ray showing congenital abnormalities of L 5 and S 1. These abnormalities impede normal spinal mobility.

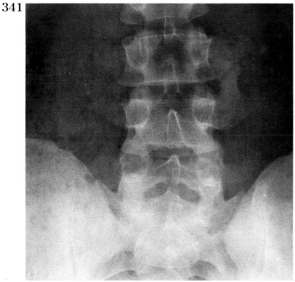

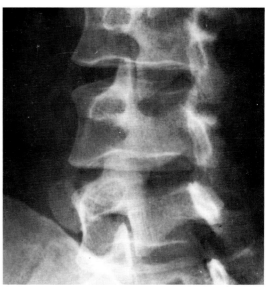

341 Intertransverse pseudarthrosis – probably congenital but it may represent old and very abnormal ectopic calcification.

342 Posterior facetal joint. Oblique radiograph showing apparent loss of posterior facetal joint L 4/5.

Most congenital spinal abnormalities are of relatively little clinical significance. Spina bifida has obvious clinical importance but the mild occult cases seldom cause probems. However, in individuals engaged in high performance activities the presence of spinal abnormalities may interfere with normal mechanical function and so provide a source of weakness and a cause of pain.

Lumbosacral strain

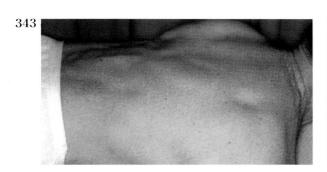

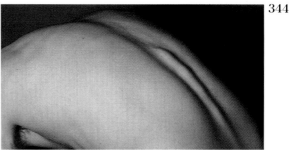

343 Spasm of the paravertebral muscles inhibiting extension, with loss of normal lumbar lordosis.

344 Spasm of the paravertebral muscles inhibiting flexion showing loss of normal prominence of spinous processes.

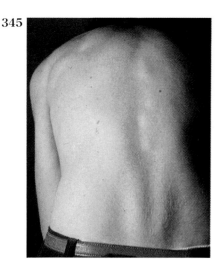

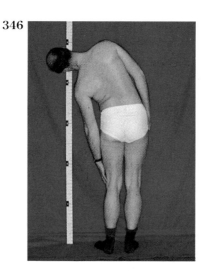

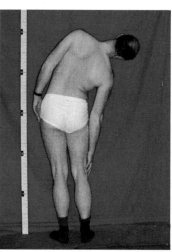

345 Spasm of paravertebral muscles causing scoliosis.

346 and **347 Asymmetry in lateral flexion** due to unilateral spasm of paravertebral muscles.

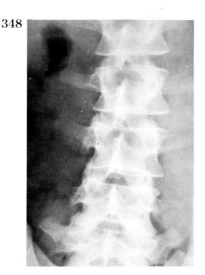

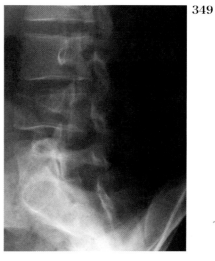

348 Vertebral rotation. This X-ray shows loss of normal contour due to vertebral rotation. Note, however, that the shape of the vertebral bodies is normal.

349 Degenerative change in a facetal joint (L 5/S 1) seen on a lateral X-ray.

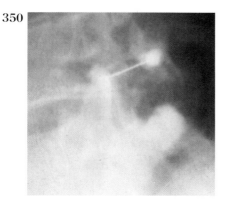

Acute lumbosacral strain is usually due to sprain of a posterior facetal joint associated with spasm and limitation of movement, but no sciatic pain or neurolgical involvement.

Abnormal spinal curvature and loss of mobility are important signs of local muscle spasm. Restoration of normal mobility using spasmolytic drugs, ice or heat, traction, manipulation and exercise, is essential to secure relief of symptoms.

350 Arthrogram of a facetal joint showing distortion of the joint distally in chronic facetal joint strain.

Ligament injuries

Ligament injuries such as sprung-back and kissing spine syndrome (hyperflexion and hyperextension injuries) seem quite rare in sport, except perhaps in diving and trampoline accidents. Usually the sportsman is fit enough to ride the stresses involved and only becomes injured with more severe stress, which tends to produce more severe injuries such as wedge fractures.

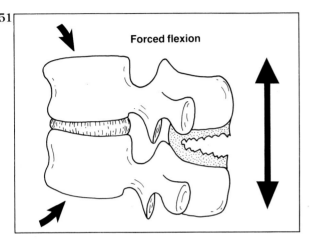

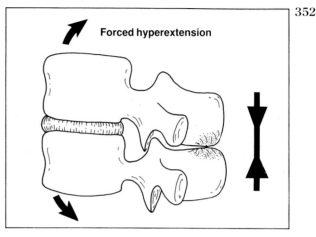

351 Sprung back – diagrammatic representation of mechanism.

352 Kissing spines – diagrammatic representation of mechanism.

Overload injuries

Loading of the spine is quite severe in some training programmes, and weight-training (as opposed to weight-lifting) is a potent cause of stress injury.

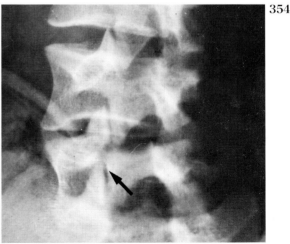

353 Lumbar spinal stress. Weight-training is a potent cause of lumbar spinal stress leading to stress fracture. Load is indicated by the bend in the bar (315 1b) handled by this female athlete.

354 Spondylolysis. Stress fracture of the pars interarticularis of L 5 showing typical 'Scottie-dog with collar' appearance on an oblique X-ray. Not always symptomatic, this may be found at random.

Treatment of spondylolysis is by immobilization to allow healing. Non-union may also require immobilization, but a remarkable number of patients seem to lose their symptoms while retaining their fractures, perhaps because of fibrous rather than bony union.

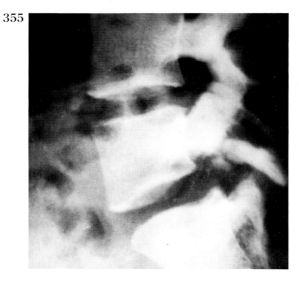

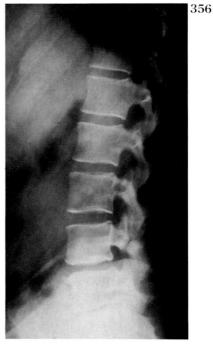

355 Spondylolysis in a tennis player. L 5/S 1 lateral radiograph.

356 Spondylolysis in an oarsman – lateral X-ray showing L 4/5.

Spondylolisthesis represents spinal instability and sport, particularly at a high level, is often impossible. Even after successful surgery to stabilize the spine, caution dictates some restriction in activity.

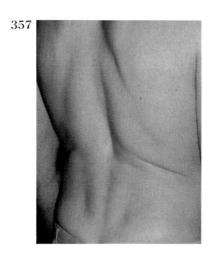

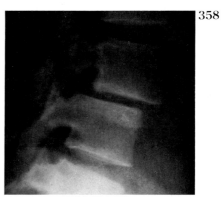

358 X-ray of 357 showing forward slip.

357 Spondylolisthesis – a clinical photograph showing a typical step in the lumbar spine of an international oarsman.

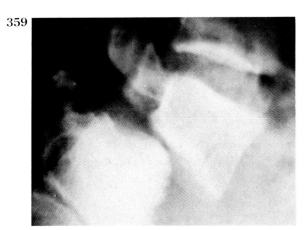

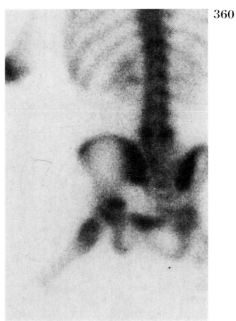

359 X-ray of L 5/S 1 spondylolisthesis with marked displacement. This patient presented with a discomfort in the thigh while running and was diagnosed previously as a chronic hamstring strain.

360 T99 scan showing 'hot nodes' at defects in the pars interarticularis.

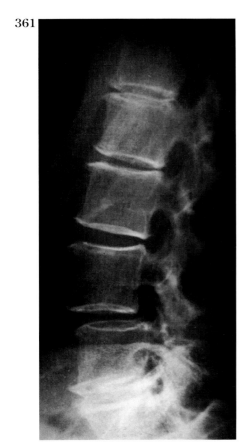

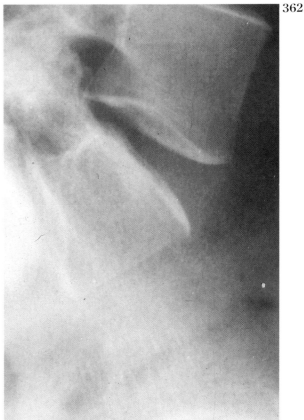

361 Pseudospondylolisthesis – forward displacement of the superior vertebral body associated with disc loss – note there is no defect in the lamina. This is a cause of low back pain in the older patient.

362 So-called 'retrolisthesis'. The superior vertebral body appears to sublux posteriorly on that below. This is probably of no clinical significance other than as a sign of paravertebral muscle spasm.

Disc lesions

Disc lesions of the spine are difficult to diagnose clinically unless clearcut criteria are accepted. It is useful to restrict this term to those conditions where there is objective evidence of neurological disturbance associated with backache and referred pain in the legs. Almost invariably in these cases, particularly in the more chronic ones, evidence of disc prolapse will be demonstrable on contrast radiography.

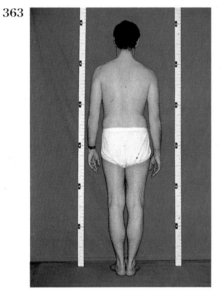

363 Typical sciatic scoliosis (associated with a disc lesion with loss of straight leg raising and neurological disturbance).

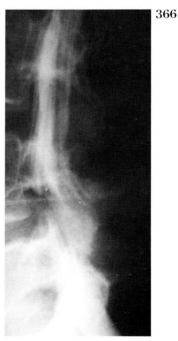

364 Disc degeneration at L 4/5.

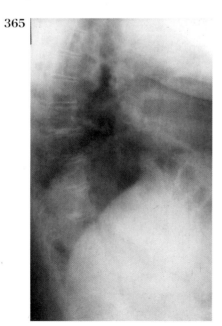

365 Degenerative discs showing calcification.

366 Disc protrusion. Lateral view of metrizamide radiculogram showing typical appearances of disc protrusion with filling defect.

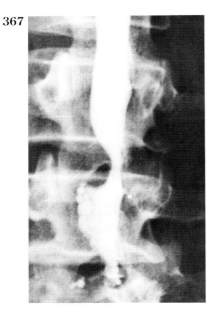

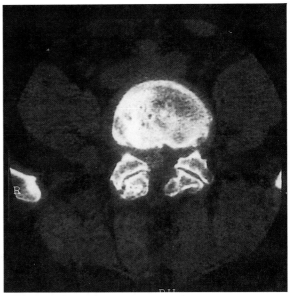

367 Disc protrusion. Oblique view of a myelogram showing typical disc protrusion.

368 Disc prolapse demonstrated on a CT scan.

If disc protrusions fail to settle rapidly exploration and removal of the prolapse are required. Return to sport should be gradual thereafter.

Degenerative changes – spinal osteochondritis

True 'growing pains' are often associated with excessive training, particularly weight training.

The changes of osteochondritis are seen as much in the dorsal as in the lumbar spine. Indeed, in Scheuermann's disease the kyphosis may be the most immediately obvious factor although many patients with this condition complain of low back pain. The main significance of the osteochondritides is that in addition to causing pain in adolescence while the disease is active, the subsequent distortion of the vertebral bodies (particularly where the patient is allowed to continue a rigorous sporting life) may predispose to degenerative joint disease at a later date.

Management is symptomatic, as the condition usually resolves with time.

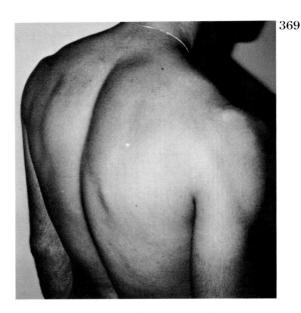

369 Scheuermann's disease – a clinical photograph showing dorsal kyphosis.

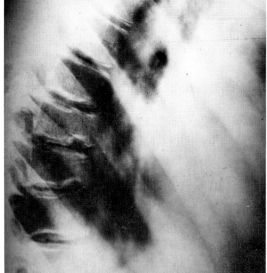

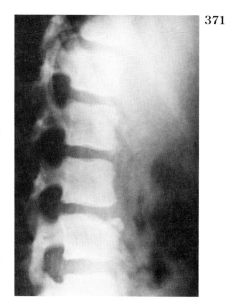

370 Scheuermann's disease – X-ray appearance.

371 Not osteochondritis but a limbus vertebra. A congenital anomaly.

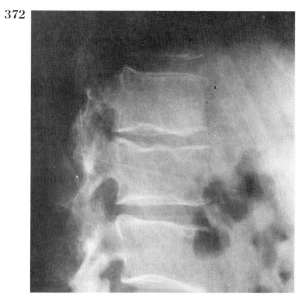

372 Osteochondritis – a lateral X-ray of an adult spine showing distortion of vertebral bodies due to old osteochondritis.

373 Osteochondritis. Gymnastic agility – hyper-extension of the spine appears to be a common cause of osteochondritis and stress fractures of the spine in young girls.

Many of these conditions appear to be exacerbated by excessive load bearing in youth – due either to overvigorous attempts at mobilization (for example, in gymnastic training) or to the too-early acceptance by the victims of heavy weight training programmes.

Generally it is advisable that loads exceeding the body weight should not be accepted as part of a weight training programme until after skeletal maturity.

Degenerative changes – spondylosis

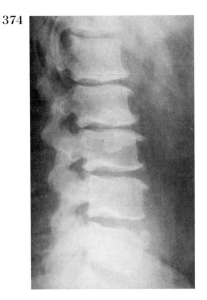

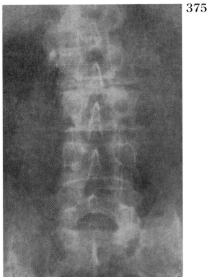

374 Spondylosis – X-ray of the spine of an international rugby player (front row forward) showing the consequences of prolonged and repeated overload.

375 Spondylosis – anteroposterior X-ray of the spine of a middle-aged international shot putter and discus thrower.

Fractures

Fractures assume major importance if there is neurological damage to the spinal cord or corda equina. Minor fractures, eg of the transverse process due to muscle violence, are of significance only in respect of disabling symptoms of pain or if visceral damage also occurs in cases involving direct violence (extrinsic injury).

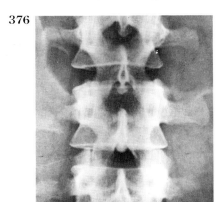

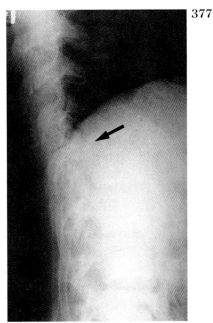

376 Fractures of transverse process caused by falling from a horse. Such fractures are occasionally due to muscle violence. In extrinsic injury the possibility of associated renal damage must be remembered.

377 Spinal fracture associated with severe violence producing instability and spinal cord injury. A catastrophe and the antithesis of all that sport intends.

Other conditions – inflammatory and neoplastic

It must always be borne in mind that inflammatory lesions and even spinal tumours may first present with pain and loss of spinal mobility associated with sport.

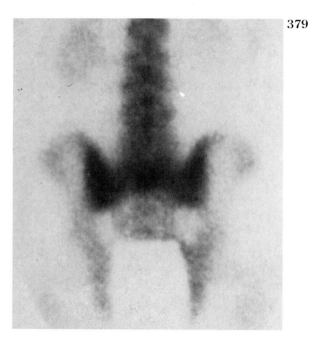

378 Ankylosing spondylitis – an X-ray showing sacroiliitis in a patient presenting with low back pain during and after sport.

379 Ankylosing spondylitis – T99 scan showing marked increase in uptake at the sacroiliac joints.

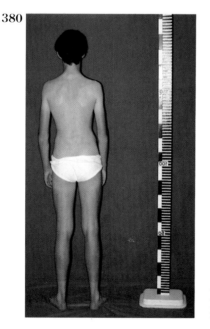

380 Gross spasm in a patient presenting with low back pain associated with sport – he was found to have a meningioma.

Sacrum and coccyx

These structures are almost injury-free in sport. Injury to the sacroiliac joint may occur in severe pelvic damage, and a genuine sacroiliac strain may be associated with traumatic osteitis pubis.

While injuries to the sacrum and coccyx are relatively uncommon except in cases of direct violence, damage to the sacroiliac joint is often described (although this may be a misinterpretation of strain of the insertion of erector spinae at the lower end over the sacroiliac joint).

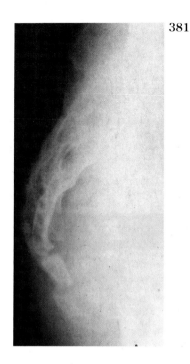

381

381 A coccygeal fracture due to a fall from a pommel-box.

11 Pelvis and hip injuries

Pelvic injuries are quite common but usually mild, being typically of the muscle origin/insertion avulsion type. More severe injury associated with direct violence occasionally occurs in vehicular accidents.

Os innominatum

382 Major pelvic injury occurs in high-velocity impacts, as in motorcycle race crashes.

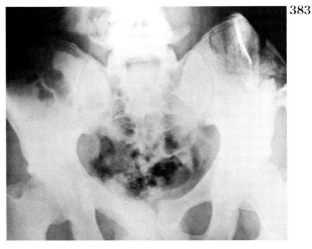

383 Major fracture due to direct violence. This type of injury occurs in riding and motor racing accidents.

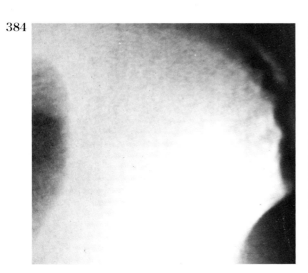

384 Avulsion of the iliac crest epiphysis. A stress injury in a young gymnast – the treatment is rest.

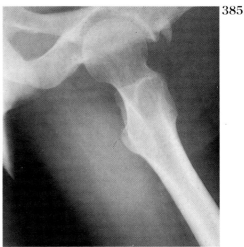

385 Avulsion injury of rectus femoris muscle origin. Quite a common injury in young boys – the treatment again is rest.

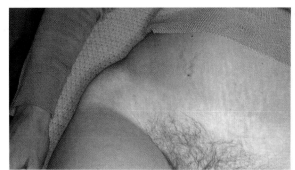

386 Haematoma on the pelvic rim due to a direct blow from a hockey stick – no underlying bone damage.

Traumatic osteitis pubis

Traumatic osteitis pubis is a tiresome condition often seen in soccer players (it is sometimes known as 'inguinocrural pain of footballers'). The patient complains of an aching pain in the groin associated with abduction of the leg. A classic feature is marked tenderness over the symphysis pubis and the differential diagnosis is from adductor ('rider's') strain. Some cases may be associated with a genuine urethritis and may be a manifestation of Reiter's syndrome. Incipient inguinal hernia may present similarly and should be excluded accordingly.

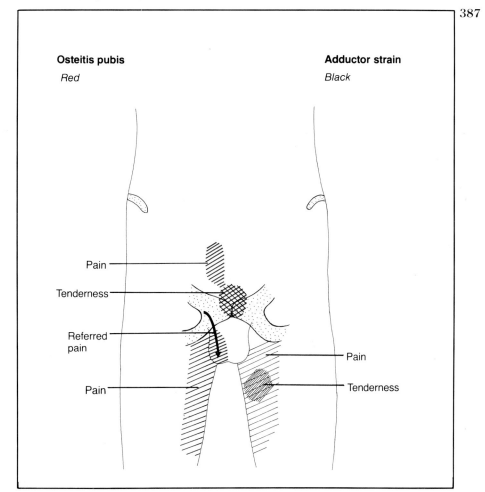

387 Sites of pain and tenderness (with differentiation from adductor strain).

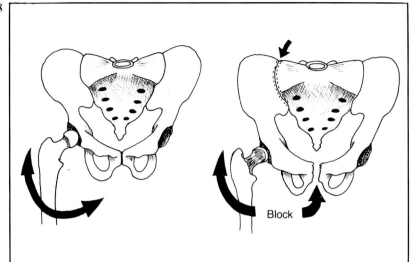

388 Mechanism of injury in extension. The inability of the distorted hip joint to rotate imposes shearing stress to the symphysis.

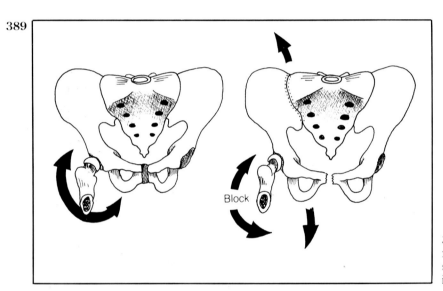

389 Mechanism of injury in flexion. In this situation the sacroiliac joints are also often involved.

390 The stress situation. The player in red (no. 10) is at risk – the player in yellow is stressing his adductors.

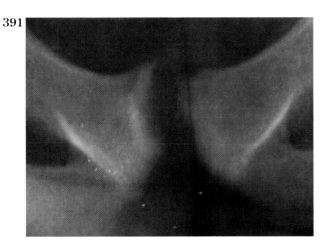

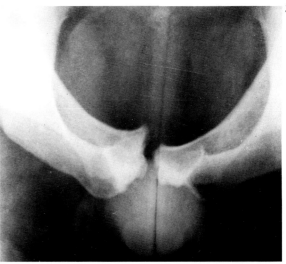

391 and **392 Traumatic osteitis pubis** – appearances of symphysis pubis.

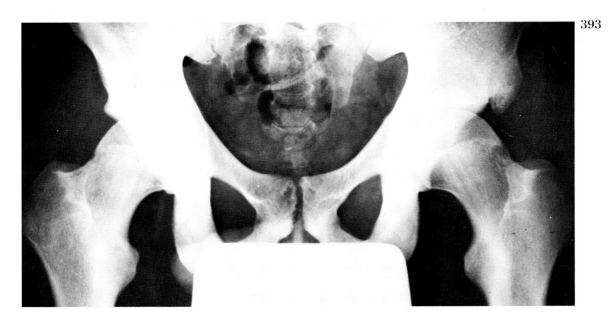

393 Pistol grip (tilt) deformity of femoral heads often associated with traumatic osteitis pubis.

Treatment is general rest, anti-inflammatory medication and hip mobilization by exercise or manipulation.

In the really resistant case, fusion of the symphysis pubis may be effective but can of itself lead to further stress due to transmission of forces onwards to the rest of the pelvis and the sacroiliac joints. Some patients show evidence, both clinical and radiological, of sacroiliac subluxation.

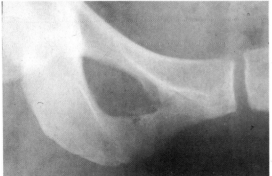

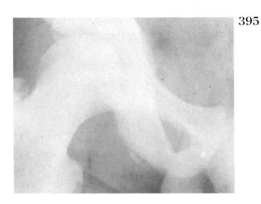

394 Stress fracture of the inferior pubic ramus in a fell runner.

395 Avulsion of adductor attachment on inferior pubic ramus.

Ischium

Most ischial injuries in sport are like other pelvic injuries, due to avulsion of the muscle attachments.

Avulsion of the hamstring is most common in the young athlete but hamstring origin strain may present at any age.

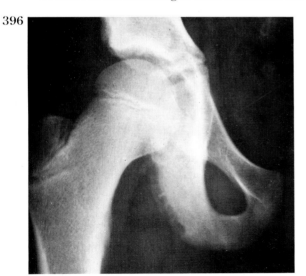

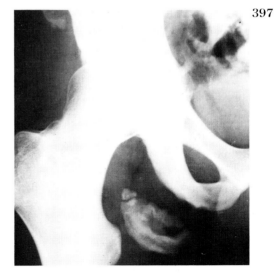

396 Hamstring tear. Radiotranslucent appearance of the ischial tuberosity associated with hamstring tear in an 11-year-old sprinter.

397 Avulsion of the ischial tuberosity in an adolescent schoolboy. Note also in this case the avulsion of the attachment of the sartorius on the same side.

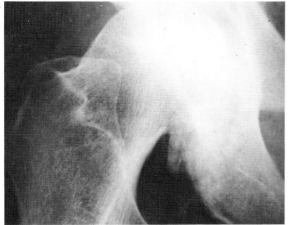

398

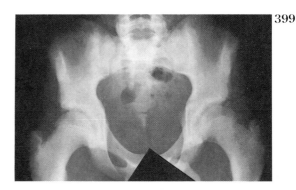

399

398 Calcification in the hamstring origin at the lateral end of the ischial tuberosity in a 40-year-old skier.

399 Fracture of the acetabular margin in a soccer player who had been tackled awkwardly and had fallen across another player's leg. He continued to play football but had persistent pain.

Muscle avulsion injuries at this site often present apparently catastrophic appearances on radiography but it is remarkable how well healing takes place with limited subsequent disability. The important

aim of treatment is to stretch and mobilize the tissues within the limits of pain tolerance from the outset.

Hip joint

Slipped upper femoral epiphysis

400

401

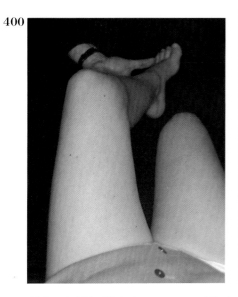

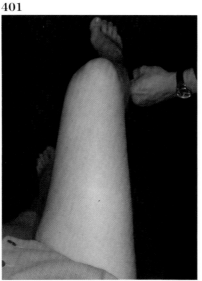

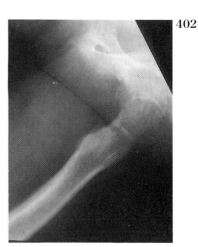

402

400 and 401 Clinical appearance of flexion deformity of the hip (**400**) in a gymnast complaining of pain in the *knee* (referred pain – the common method of presentation). The extension of the hip is normal on the unaffected side (**401**).

402 A lateral X-ray of the hip in slipped upper femoral epiphysis – the slip will often fail to show on the anteroposterior view.

Perthe's disease – pseudocoxalgia

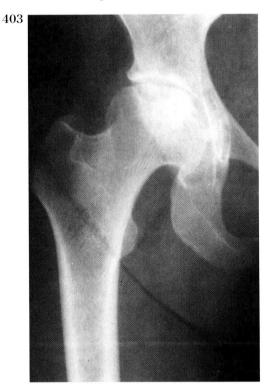

403 Pseudocoxalgia. This condition normally presents as knee pain. Osteochondritis of the upper femoral epiphysis may lead to severe distortion of the femoral head and early degenerative joint disease.

MORAL: Always examine the hip of any child presenting with gradual onset of knee pain – *particularly* if there are no obvious knee signs.

Dislocation of the hip joint

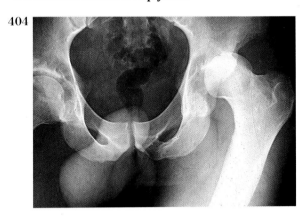

404 Dislocation of the hip – the result of a fall from a horse with the foot trapped in the stirrup.

This predisposes to premature onset of degenerative joint disease such as osteoarthrosis.

Degenerative joint disease – osteoarthrosis

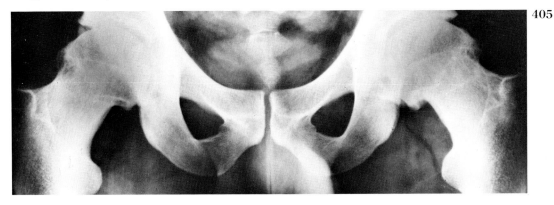

405 Severe degenerative joint disease associated with marked limitation of hip movements in an individual still playing rugby league football as a professional.

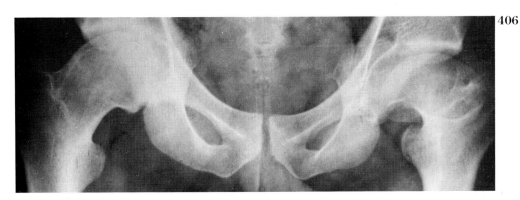

406 Dysplasia. Marked dysplasia of the hip in a professional golfer (note also the deformity in the other hip). Pain and discomfort in the hip during the second round of golf played in the day led to this individual abandoning tournament golf.

Fracture of the femur

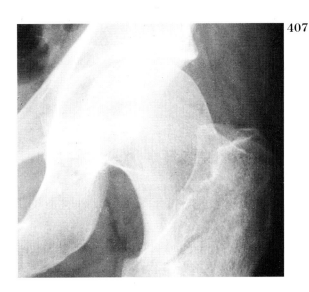

407 X-ray of a fracture of the femur (inter-trochanteric) in a soccer player who had fallen onto his left hip on a hard ground. He complained that the hip was sore, but he was still able to walk without discomfort.

Stress fractures

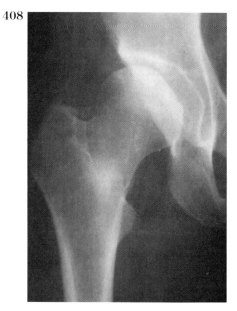

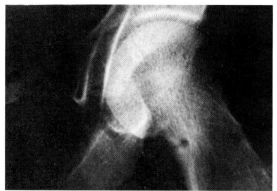

409 Stress fracture of the femoral neck in a young badminton player.

408 Stress fracture of the femoral neck following a first marathon run.

Ectopic calcification

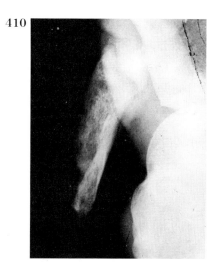

410 Ectopic calcification in sartorius strain – X-ray appearance.

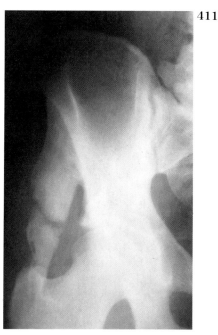

411 Ectopic calcification in gluteus medius.

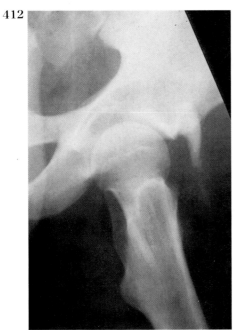

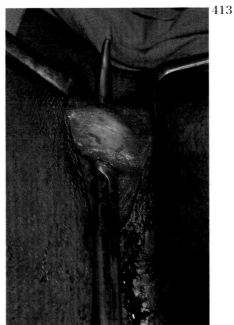

412 Ectopic calcification in rectus femoris due to repeated avulsion stress (note the shape of the bony deposit). This player resumed his international rugby career after excision of the bone.

413 Excision of ectopic bone and tenotomy in a soccer player with ectopic calcification in the adductor.

Regeneration of the bone does not seem to occur if removal of the calcification is delayed until the bone is fully mature.

Tumour

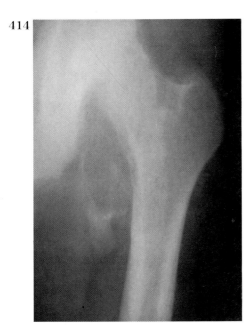

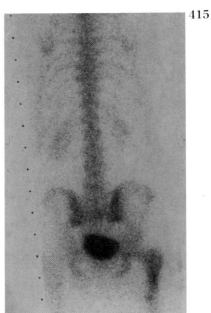

414 A calcifying chondrosarcoma, not ectopic calcification as had been suggested. Note the early erosion of the femoral cortex. Tomogram.

415 A bone scan of 414 clearly shows the involvement of the upper femur.

Soft-tissue injury

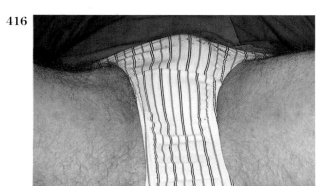

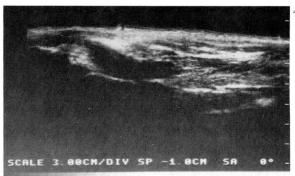

416 Psoas bursa – the clinical appearance, showing swelling anterior to the adductor tendons in the right groin.

417 Psoas bursa demonstrated on an ultrasound scan.

Muscle injury: adductor strain (rider's strain)

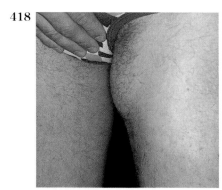

418 Large adductor haematoma in acute rider's strain.

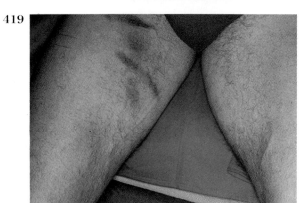

419 Ecchymosis in acute adductor strain – diffuse as in all muscle tears.

12 Thigh injuries

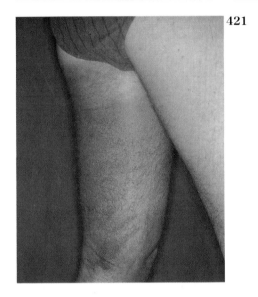

420

420 Ecchymosis due to direct violence (skiing) – well localized to the site of the blow.

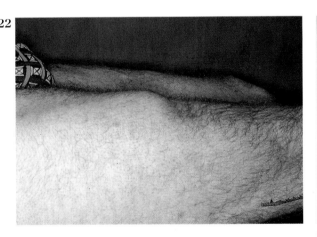

421

421 Ecchymosis due to interstitial hamstring tear – this looks dramatic but is of little significance as energetic early mobilization procures rapid resolution.

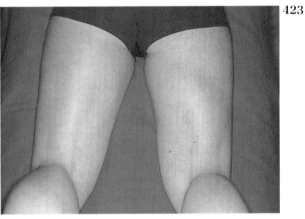

422

423

422 Complete rupture of rectus femoris showing a bulge at the proximal retracted stump of muscle on contraction.

423 Complete hamstring tear – biceps. There is no indication for surgical intervention since such repair usually fails and full function is normally restored with no more than energetic mobilization and stretching. Complete hamstring rupture occurs in baseball players.

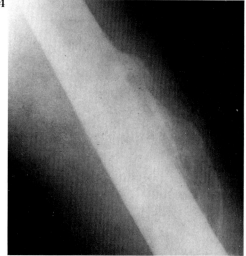

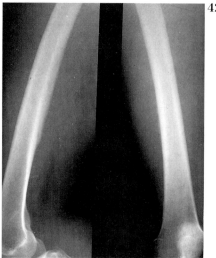

424 Ectopic calcification – myositis ossificans in the vastus intermedius due to a direct blow on the front of the thigh – 'corked thigh' or 'charleyhorse'. Note that the femoral cortex is intact and calcification is in the soft tissue only.

425 Stress fracture of the shaft of the femur – another first-time marathon runner!

Iliotibial band syndromes

426
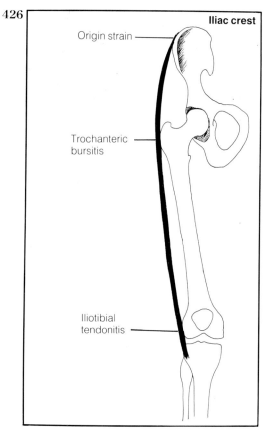

426 Sites of injury in iliotibial band syndromes. Injury to the iliotibial band (tensor fascia lata) may occur as an avulsion from the origin on the iliac crest, as peritendonitis associated with trochanteric bursitis, as a muscle pull, or as a tendonitis or bursitis over the lateral femoral condyle.

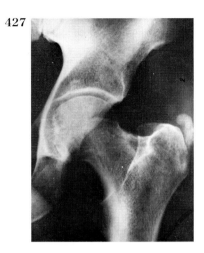

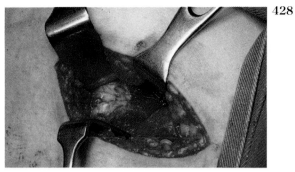

428 Ectopic calcification in gluteus medius tendon at operation.

427 Ectopic calcification in gluteus medius tendon (trochanteric bursitis).

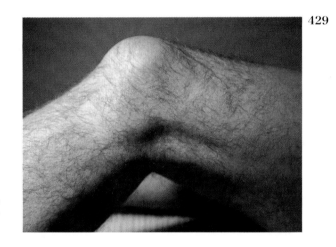

429 Iliotibial band syndrome – a swollen bursa deep to the iliotibial band, appearing behind the posterior border of the latter.

13 Knee joint injuries

The knee joint is the most vulnerable joint in sport since it is inherently unstable and fully weight-bearing. The complexity of the joint ensures a wide variety of different clinical problems, and this in turn tends to produce difficulty in diagnosis. In some instances, patients suffering from knee injury do not get the correct initial treatment and present later with degenerative joint diseases.

Congenital abnormalities

For mechanical reasons all these abnormalities make the knee more vulnerable to trauma.

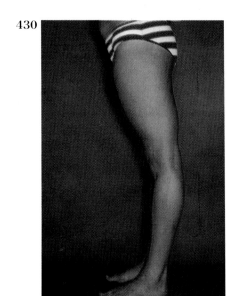

430 Genu recurvatum – hyper-extension of the knee, often associated with hypermobile joint disease, and sometimes a cause of recurrent patellar dislocation.

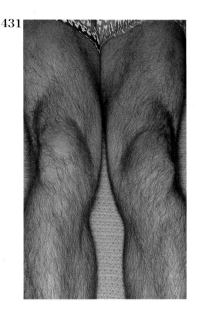

431 Genu valgum – knock-knees, a predisposing factor in chondro-malacia patellae.

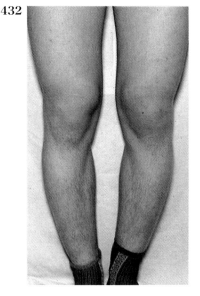

432 Genu varum – bow-legs, often associated with torsion of the tibia.

As in the case of the elbow joint, varus, valgus and recurvatus deformity of the knee can impose additional mechanical stresses on the joint, in particular on the extensor apparatus – which, in a sportsman, may lead to the production of symptoms. Management may be difficult. In many instances it may be necessary to divert the patient to a more biomechanically suitable form of sporting activity.

433 Congenital abnormalities may also affect soft tissue – here, a supernumerary third head of biceps crosses the lateral side of the knee joint, causing a friction syndrome similar to iliotibial band syndrome.

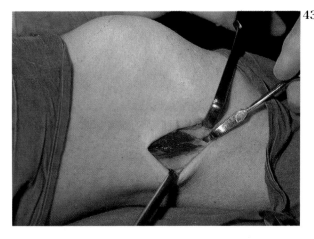

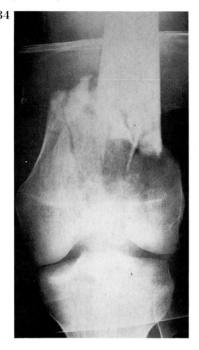

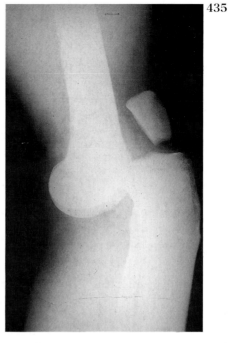

434 A catastrophic fracture in a skiing accident – return to the sport is unlikely.

435 Comprehensive dislocation in a rugby accident. The popliteal nerves and vessels are at risk in an accident of this type.

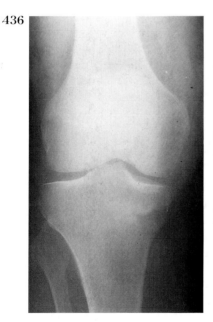

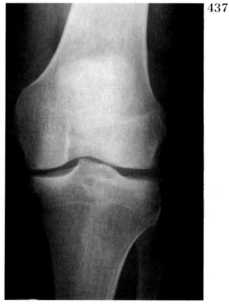

436 Tibial plateau or bumper fracture. Return to sport is problematic as perfect realignment of the joint surface is almost impossible.

437 Marginal fractures. Although bone damage is slight, pain and disability can be severe. These fractures are readily missed and oblique views may be necessary to demonstrate them.

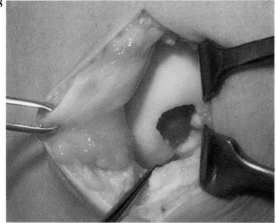

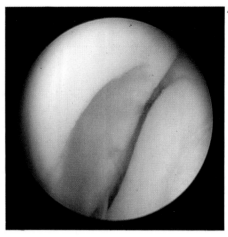

438 Erosion of the femoral condyle in a patient with osteochondral fracture. This is often similar in presentation and behaviour to osteochondritis dissecans – but follows acute trauma.

439 Healing erosion – arthroscopic view. Resumption of sport should present no problems but the risk of later degenerative change is enhanced.

Osteochondritis dissecans

Osteochondritis dissecans is an important cause of pain in the knee in adolescent sportsmen. In fact, patients do surprisingly well with defects after separation (and removal) of an osteochondritic fragment. Minimal interference is the optimum line of treatment.

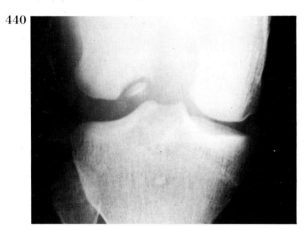

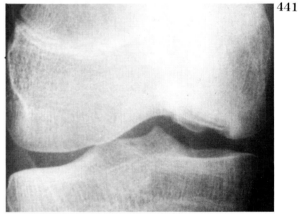

440 Condylar defect – an X-ray of the knee, showing marked condylar defect and loose body formation.

441 Fragmentation – an X-ray of the knee, showing a less well-marked defect and early development of separating fragment. At this stage, fixing the fragment may promote reattachment and subsequent healing.

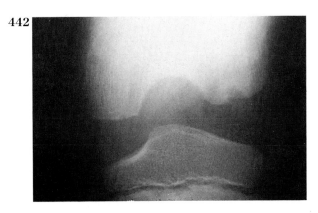

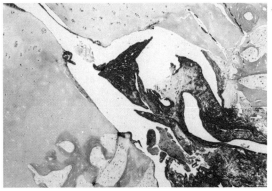

442 Osteochondritis may affect either femoral condyle or, as in this case, both.

443 Histology of osteochondritic fragment.

Degenerative joint disease

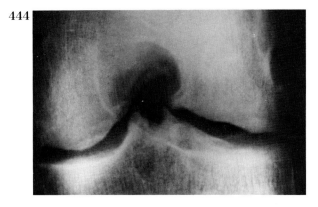

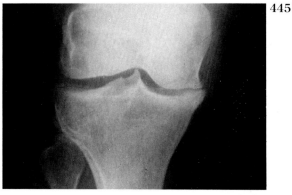

444 Osteoarthritis associated with a previous history of osteochondritis dissecans in an international weight-lifter.

445 Osteoarthrosis of the knee joint in a 32-year-old professional tennis player who previously had numerous injuries and a complete medial meniscectomy.

Osteoarthrosis of the knee joint is relatively common at an early age in sportsmen, and is typically associated with inadequate or unsuitable earlier management of a primary knee injury. It is therefore clearly important that all knee injuries should be taken seriously and treated and rehabilitated effectively to prevent the early onset of degenerative joint disease.

Injury to ligaments and capsule

Collateral ligament injury

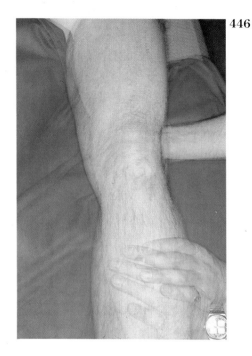

446 Lateral ligament rupture – a superimposition photograph showing a varus defect in the knee on application of adduction stress.

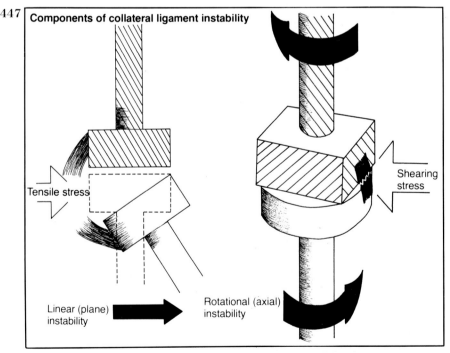

447 Mechanism of ligament injury. Direct stress across a ligament may be coupled with rotational strain to give rotary instability.

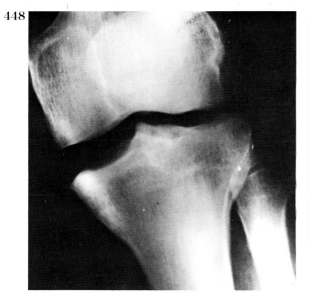

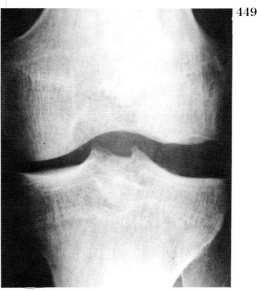

448 Medial ligament tear – a stress X-ray showing the medial side of the joint opening up in a medial ligament tear.

449 Lateral ligament tear – a stress X-ray showing the lateral side of the joint opening up in a lateral ligament tear. (Sometimes confused with lateral ligament strain is **popliteus tenosynovitis**. This condition is virtually incapable of illustration. The clinical features are pain on running downhill and on sitting with legs crossed.)

Cruciate ligament injury

Cruciate ligament damage can cause severe biomechanical disturbance in the knee. The cruciates control not only anteroposterior movement at the knee joint but also the pivot point for rotation during the lock-home phase of extension. Damage to either cruciate, particularly when associated with capsular damage, is a potent factor of rotary instability of the knee and pivot shift.

Established instability demands surgical repair. Many procedures are available for reconstruction of the anterior cruciate ligament – reconstruction of the posterior cruciate ligament in late cases is less immediately effective but alternative dynamic stabilization procedures are available which allow resumption of normal sporting activity.

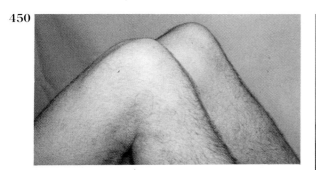

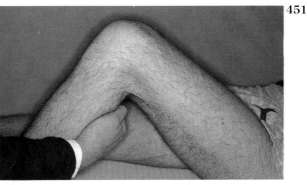

450 Posterior cruciate injury showing typical deformity of posterior drawer sign in left knee.

451 Anterior cruciate injury – the anterior drawer sign showing the tibia pulling forward in relation to the femoral condyles. This sign is only positive if the tibia pulls forward with the lower leg *internally* rotated.

452

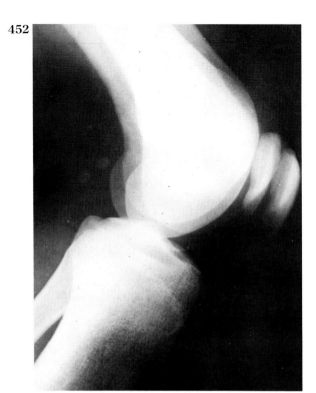

452 Anterior cruciate ligament tear – the superimposed lateral X-ray shows instability in a cruciate ligament tear.

Pellegrini-Stieda's disease

Calcification is present in all cases. When symptomatic, local steroid injection usually cures.

453

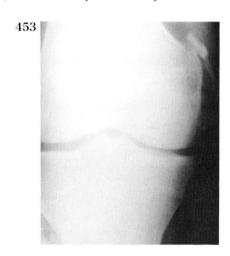

454

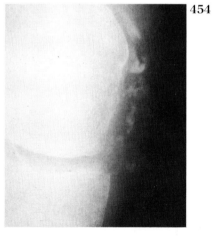

453 Ectopic calcification in the upper attachment of the medial collateral ligament is sometimes a sequel of injury. The X-ray appearances are variable.

454 Pellegrini-Stieda's disease – a variant.

Coronary ligament strain. Occasionally the coronary ligaments binding the menisci to the upper surface of the tibia may be strained. Symptoms are similar to meniscus tear, but without locking, and tenderness is below the joint line. Treatment is conservative.

Traumatic synovitis

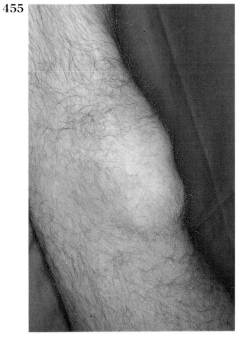

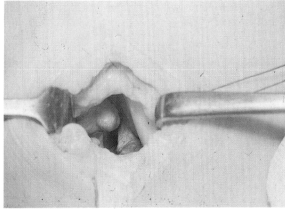

456 Damage to the alar folds with nipping and tag formation may mimic meniscus tear, with apparent locking in some cases. Arthroscopy may be required to differentiate, and grossly hypertrophic alar folds may need surgical excision.

455 Inflammation of the retropatellar fat pad (Hoffa's disease). Swelling below the patella on either side of the patellar tendon may follow repeated (negative) arthroscopies.

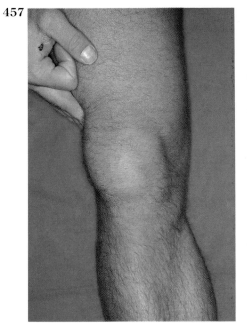

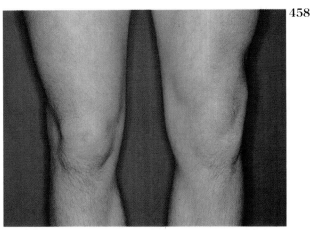

458 Large volume haemarthrosis due to trauma to the alar folds or anterior cruciate ligament.

457 Low volume serous effusion in synovitis. The fluid may be 'milked' from one side of the patella to the other.

Knee injury – meniscus

Injury to the menisci due to rotational strain in the flexed weight-bearing knee is extremely common.

Differential diagnosis and management of the injuries are according to standard orthopaedic practice.

Main types of meniscus tear

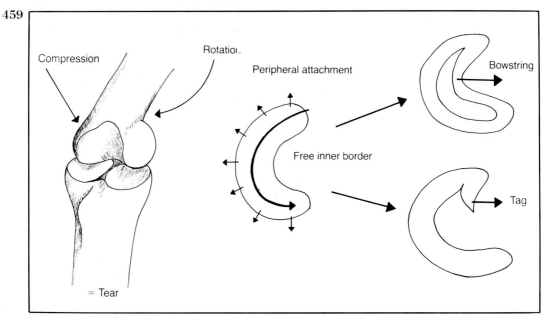

459 Mechanism of knee injury. Rotational stress on the flexed weight-bearing knee.

Bucket handle or 'bowstring' tear (medial meniscus)

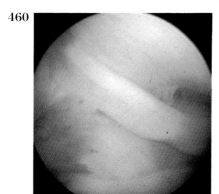

460 Tear as seen at arthroscopy.

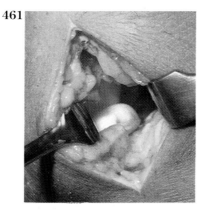

461 Tear as seen at operation for removal of detached portion.

462 Meniscectomy specimen showing longitudinal split. If periphery of meniscus is intact, only detached fragment need be removed.

Tag or 'parrot beak' tear (post horn of medial meniscus)

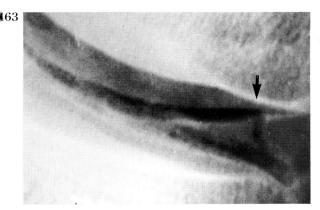

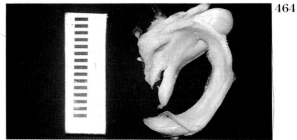

464 Tear as seen in an operation specimen.

463 Tear as seen at arthrogram.

465

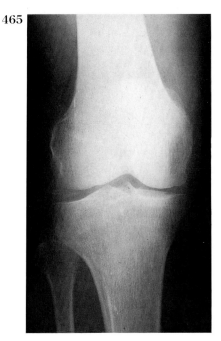

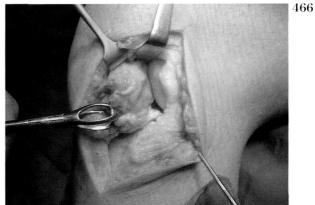

466

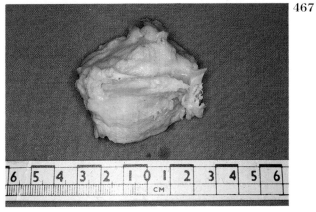

467

465 Chondrocalcinosis. Meniscus degeneration with ectopic calcification.

Meniscus tears are often associated with ligament damage, the effects of which are sometimes exacerbated by meniscectomy.

466 and 467 The site of an intracapsular meniscal cyst with attachment to meniscus and (**467**) the specimen. This caused a swelling medial to the patellar tendon in the patient, a golfer.

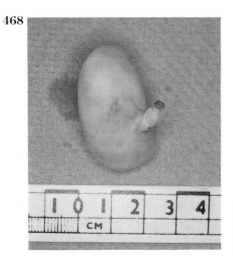

468 A pedunculated loose body (a fibroma) from the knee joint. Note the surface shape where it was opposed to the femoral condyle. This was a cause of unexplained pain and swelling in a soccer referee's knee.

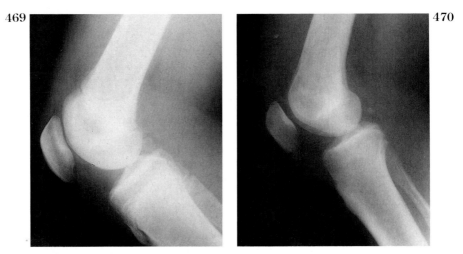

469 and **470 Loose body of unknown origin in the posterior compartment of the knee** of a young soccer player. Compare with the position of fabella (**470**).

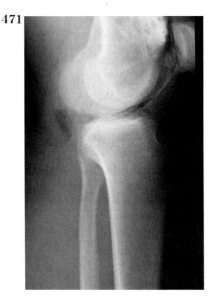

471 Loose body in the anterior compartment of the knee demonstrated on an arthrogram.

Swellings at the knee joint

Swellings outside the knee joint are quite common and may cause confusion.

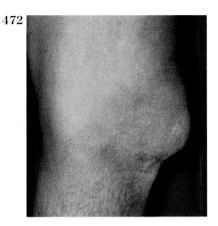

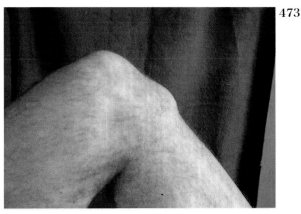

472 Pre-patellar bursitis (housemaid's knee). This is often traumatic and may develop as a result of an abrasion on hard ground or a wrestling mat.

473 Pre-patellar bursitis – in this variation, the bursa lies anterior to the anterior tibial tubercle.

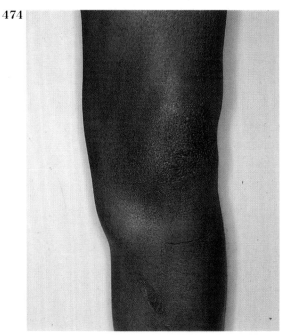

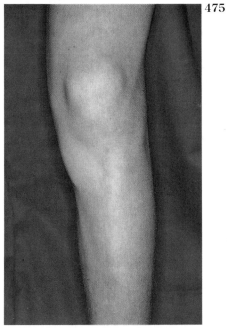

474 An adventitious anserine bursa overlying a benign exostosis which is hard to palpation.

475 True anserine bursitis or 'breaststroker's knee' – an overuse injury soft to palpation.

476

477

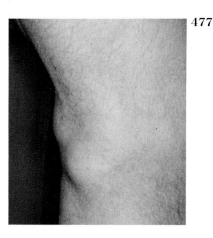

476 and **477 Popliteal cysts** (so-called 'Baker's cyst' or gastrocnemius bursa). The cyst may arise as a pouch from the posterior capsule of the knee (**476**) (with which it may communicate), or it may be associated with the semimembranous tendon or gastrocnemius (**477**). Differential diagnosis is from popliteal aneurysm which pulsates.

478

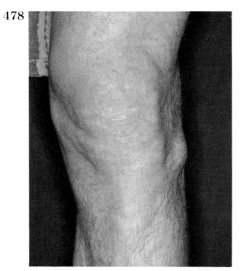

479

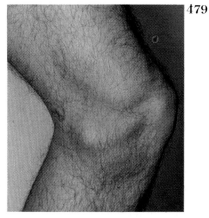

478 and **479 Cystic meniscus.** This condition is commonly found on the lateral side, but occasionally it occurs on the medial side (**479**).

480

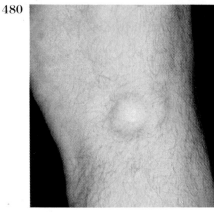

481

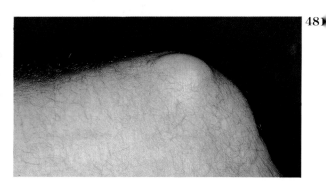

481 Another oddity – a sebaceous cyst! Common conditions may occur in uncommon places.

480 An oddity – a 'ganglion' or bursa associated with the superior tibiofibular joint which could be mistaken for a cyst of lateral meniscus.

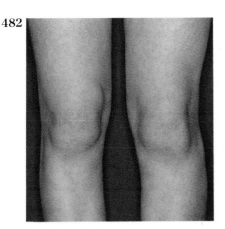

482 Sesamoid – a solid one. A prominent fibular head with an accessory ossicle (sesamoid) in the biceps tendon.

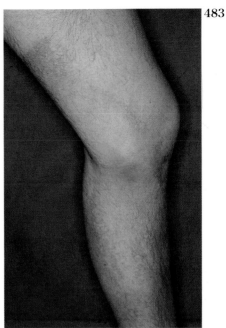

483 An encysted haematoma, a swelling of sudden onset on the medial aspect of the knee due to direct violence.

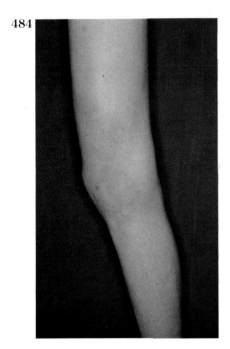

484 A cavernous haemangioma, a swelling of insidious onset on the lateral aspect of the knee.

Aspiration of cystic swellings is not recommended, due to the liability of loculation resulting, except as a 'one-off' emergency procedure.

These conditions are essentially benign and need no treatment other than reassurance, unless there is interference with mechanical function or pain due to tension in a cyst, when surgical removal may be required.

14 Patella injuries

Chondromalacia

Chondromalacia patellae is very common in sportsmen and women with males more commonly affected than females (a reversal of the ratio in the normal population). The condition is typically associated with impaired function of the extensor apparatus of the knee and is relatively easily treated provided its biomechanical basis is understood.

Chondromalacia may be quite protean in its presentation and may mimic a variety of other conditions including meniscus tear. It is also commonly present in association with the latter, as well as with other conditions such as chronic traumatic synovitis, etc.

485

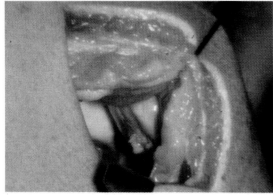

485 Undersurface of the patella at arthrotomy, showing typical degenerative change. The changes are to be regarded merely as an indicator of altered patellofemoral biomechanics and are of no significance in symptom production. Attempts to treat chondromalacia patellae by direct intervention on the undersurface of the patella are therefore unrewarding.

486

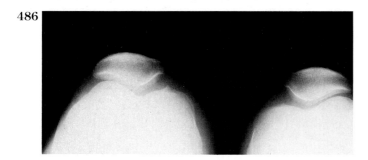

486 Skyline X-ray showing typical lateral tilt of subluxation of the patella associated with chondromalacia patellae.

487

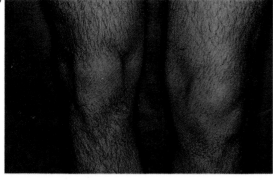

487 Vastus medialis wasting – a cardinal feature of chondromalacia patellae. This is a product of an inability fully to extend the knee, which is in turn a consequence of any form of irritation of the knee joint, slight effusion or synovitis. The vicious circle of symptom production in chrondromalacia with vastus medialis wasting and loss of normal patellofemoral joint congruity is clearly established as a result of even minor knee injuries.

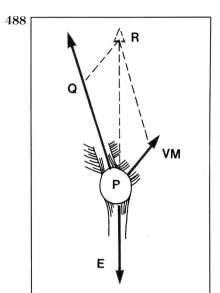

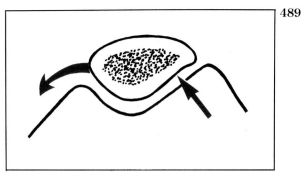

488 and **489 Biomechanics of extension.** In **488** the angle QPR is the Q angle. Note that with the knee extended the pull of the vastus medialis (VM) counteracts the tendency of the patella to displace laterally in extension; the resultant of the forces of the pull on the quadriceps tendon and the VM lies in the axis of patella tendon (E). In **489**, stabilization of the patella is partly passive by the lateral condylar ridge.

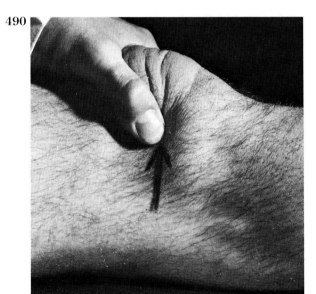

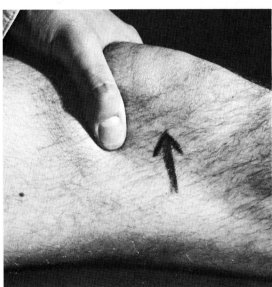

490 and **491 Clarke's sign.** First the leg is fully extended and the patient is told to relax. The patella is then pressed downwards and distally onto the patellofemoral groove (**490**), and the patient experiences pain when the quadriceps is contracted (**491**) (the patient should be warned to contract the quadriceps gently). This sign is pathognomonic of chrondromalacia patellae.

Apart from trauma causing quadriceps inhibition, predisposing factors include the following:

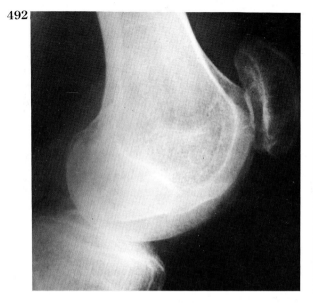

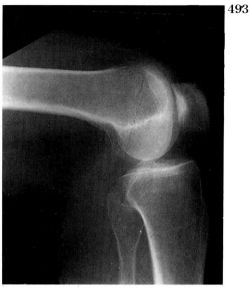

492 Patella alta – long patella tendon. The patella rides so high it loses the passive stabilization by the lateral condylar ridge.

493 Patella baja – short patella tendon. Another cause of anterior knee pain.

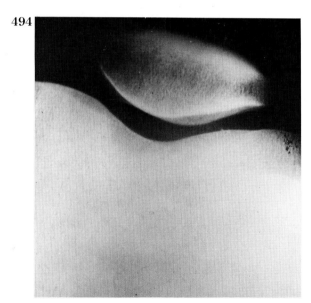

494 Small patella (often with recurrent dislocation). Note that the patella fails to engage properly on the (in this case shallow) femoral articular surface.

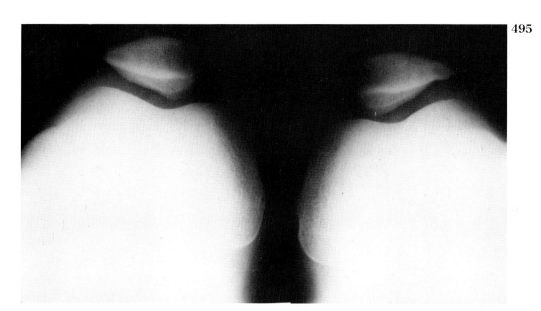

495 Abnormal shape (eg Wiberg type III with virtually no medial condylar facet). The pull of the quadriceps tends to 'squint' the patella laterally.

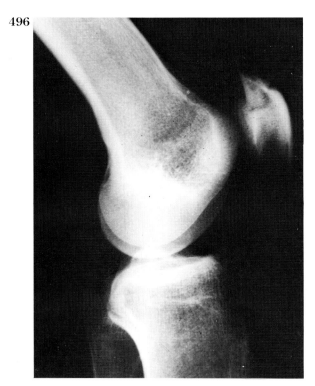

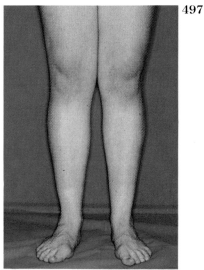

497 Genu valgum. The increased valgus angle in extension (Q angle) multiplies the resultant tendency to displace the patella laterally (parallelogram of forces). Note pronation of feet.

496 Bipartite patella – the accessory fragment is notoriously prone to malacic changes (**505**).

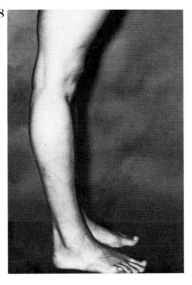

498

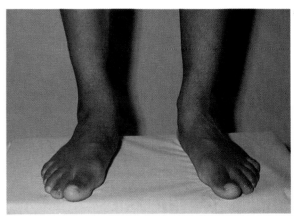

499

499 Excessive pronation of the foot with internal rotation of the lower leg and functional increase in the Q angle.

498 Genu recurvatum. The patella loses its seating on the lower end of the femur in hyperextension.

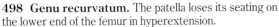

500

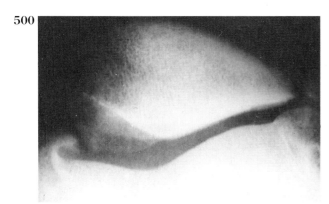

500 Osteoarthrosis of the patellofemoral joint in a soccer player with a long history of chondromalacia patellae. This is the ultimate outcome of inadequate treatment.

The presence of any of these conditions will materially affect the biomechanics of the extensor apparatus, tending to increase the Q angle and facilitate subluxation of the patella.

Conservative management

501

501 Vigorous static quadriceps contraction restores the vastus medialis. Since the vastus medialis only functions effectively in full or nearly full extension, it can only be exercised fully with the knee extended.

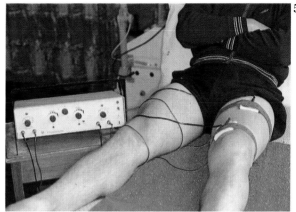

502 Vastus medialis. Occasionally this muscle is severely inhibited. Feedback may be secured by Faradic stimulation – including sequential Faradism, in which the vastus medialis is stimulated slightly in advance of the main mass of the quadriceps.

Surgical management

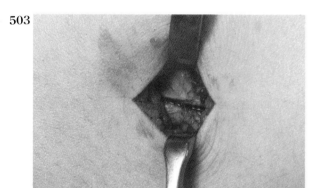
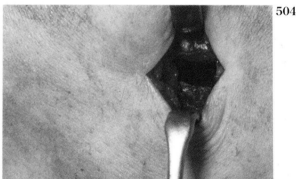

503 and **504 Lateral retinacular release.** This is the simplest procedure, whether carried out through a small incision on the lateral side of the knee or through an arthroscopy incision. In **504** the capsulotomy is completed. Note the gap as a result of the medial shift of the patella.

Other biomechanically sound procedures, anterior tibial transposition, for example, may be helpful. Procedures such as drilling the bone, patellar shave, and even patellectomy, are not biomechanically sound and results are frequently poor.

Chondromalacia patellae is one of the commonest complaints in sport and represents up to 10 per cent of all problems seen in sports injuries clinics. It is relatively easy to treat provided its biomechanical cause is understood, but it is remarkable how commonly the condition is inadequately managed and patients persist with symptoms. The condition is most notorious when it presents in adolescent and late-teenage girls, particularly those who are somewhat endomorphic and have a tendency to genu valgum. Too often these patients come finally to patellectomy as a result of inadequate early management and the results are monotonously disappointing. In the early cases, shortwave diathermy together with appropriate muscle re-education will normally produce the required relief of symptoms. Lateral retinacular release (**503** and **504**) should be regarded as the primary surgical treatment of choice in the patient who fails to respond to conservative management.

Patella – bipartite

This development anomaly is sometimes confused with a fracture. Typically it involves the upper outer pole of the patella. The articular surface of the fragment is often malacic and associated with recalcitrant symptoms.

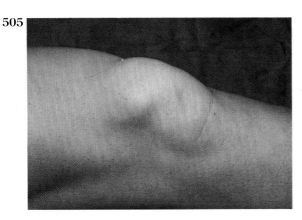

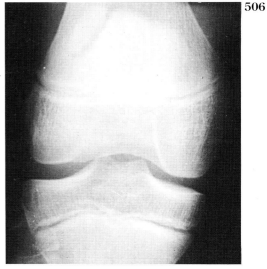

505 Patella showing visible and palpable boss on the superolateral aspect.

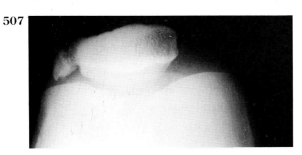

506 Anteroposterior X-ray view of the patella. Not to be confused with a fracture!

507 Skyline X-ray showing displacement of accessory fragment.

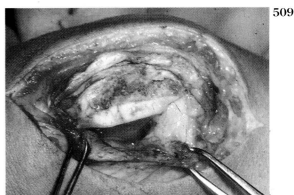

508 and **509 Appearance at operation for removal of the fragment.** Most cases are untroubled by symptoms, but when these occur the patient should be managed as for chondromalacia patellae. Excision of the fragment combined with lateral retinacular release is valuable in recalcitrant cases.

Osteochondritis

Osteochondritis of the patella is relatively uncommon but it is seen as a form of traction epiphysitis (Sinding–Larsen–Johanssen syndrome), and also as osteochondritis dissecans affecting the articular surface.

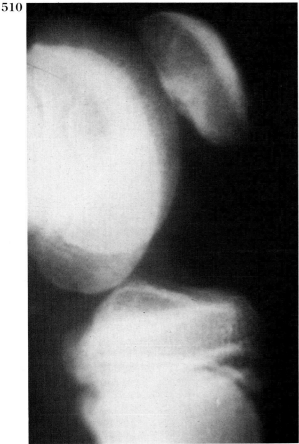

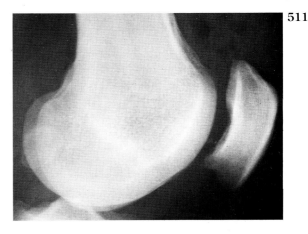

511 Osteochondritis dissecans – a lateral X-ray showing a defect on the posterior surface of the patella and a loose body visible in the posterior compartment of the knee between the femoral condyles. Treatment is excision of the loose body. The defect in the patella can usually be left alone.

510 Osteochondritis dissecans – a lateral X-ray showing a lesion on the articular surface of the patella with no separation.

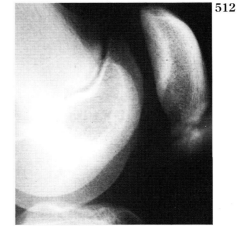

512 Sinding–Larsen–Johanssen disease showing typical appearances of osteochondritis at the lower pole of the patella. This is a condition often associated with overuse, and the treatment is rest. It is the juvenile equivalent of jumper's knee.

Fracture of the patella

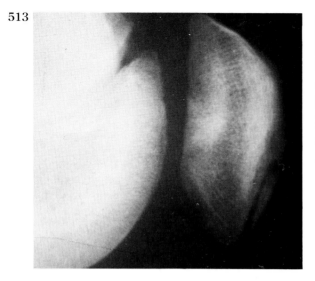

513 Stress fracture of the lower pole of the patella showing avulsion of the superficial cortex.

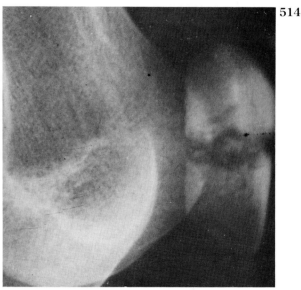

514 Fracture of the patella shown on a lateral X-ray. Fracture is due to indirect violence, ie the pull of the quadriceps apparatus. This patient returned to international soccer after excision of the distal fragment and reconstruction of the capsule and extensor apparatus.

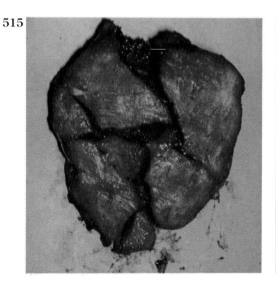

515 A comminuted fracture of the patella due to direct violence. Attempts at reduction and realignment of fragments with or without fixation are seldom as successful as patellectomy. The latter will, however, usually effectively preclude further body-contact sport.

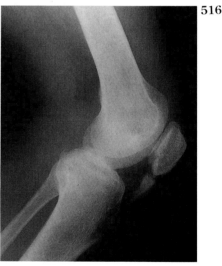

516 Ectopic calcification in the patella tendon after lower pole fracture.

Dislocation of the patella

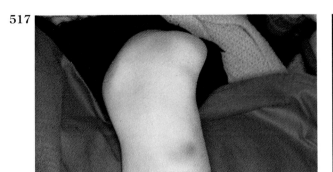

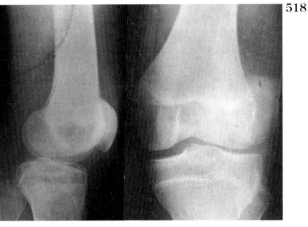

517 Clinical appearance of dislocation – note the obvious deformity. The dislocation is usually easy to reduce as long as the knee can be extended.

518 X-ray appearance of dislocation. A similar confusing appearance may be suggested in anteroposterior X-rays of the knee which are not well centred. Predisposing factors in patellar dislocation are, not surprisingly, the same as those for chondromalacia patellae (**492–499**).

Patella tendon

Patella tendonitis – jumper's knee

Patella tendonitis is common in sports involving much jumping and is characterized by pain and tenderness below the knee cap and over the patella tendon.

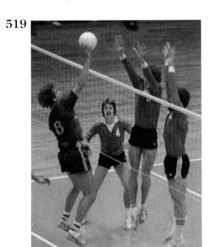

519, 520 and 521 Examples of sports involving jumping: 519 volley ball; **520** basketball; and **521** athletics.

522

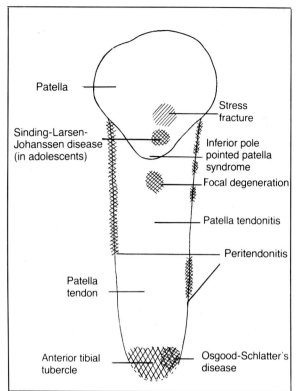

Patella

Sinding-Larsen-
Johanssen disease
(in adolescents)

Stress
fracture

Inferior pole
pointed patella
syndrome

Focal degeneration

Patella tendonitis

Peritendonitis

Patella
tendon

Anterior tibial
tubercle

Osgood-Schlatter's
disease

522 Differential diagnosis of patella tendon pain.

523

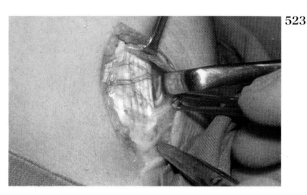

523 Peritendonitis of the patella tendon. Note the adhesions between the tendon and the surrounding tissues.

524

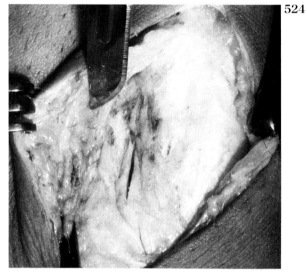

524 Tendonitis of the patella tendon. The tendon is diffusely thickened and tender.

525

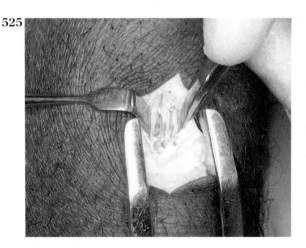

525 Focal degeneration of the patella tendon. A lesion demonstrated at operation (decathlete).

526

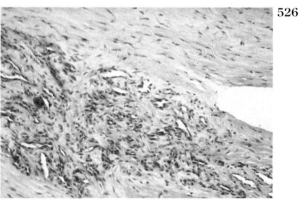

526 Histology of patella tendon focal degeneration. Note the typical 'wet tissue paper' appearance with increased cells and new blood vessel formation.

527 Prominent lower pole – 'inferior pole pointed syndrome'. Clinically, this is similar to 'jumper's knee', presenting with tenderness at the lower pole of the patella.

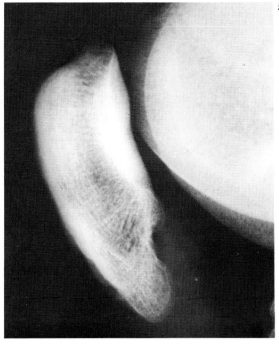

These conditions may respond to conservative treatment, eg anti-inflammatory medication, ultrasonics or shortwave diathermy. Recalcitrant cases require surgical exploration. Chondromalacia patellae is a frequent complication.

Patella tendon insertion

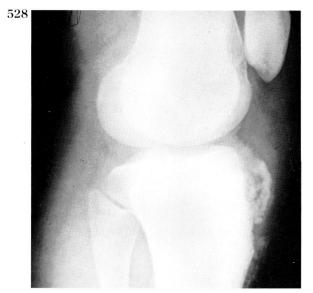

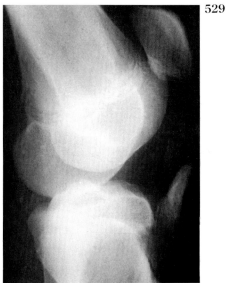

528 Osgood-Schlatter's disease, possibly due to excessive tension in the patella tendon insertion on the epiphysis of the anterior tibial tubercle in adolescence, as a result of overtraining. Note the fragmentation of the epiphysis. In some cases these separated fragments may have to be surgically removed to secure relief of pain.

529 Avulsion of the anterior tibial tubercle. The consequence of acute overloading.

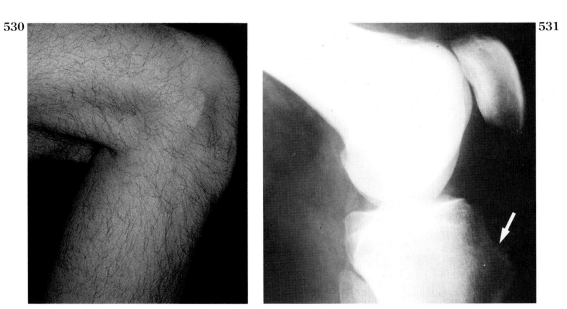

530 and **531** **Old Osgood-Schlatter's disease.** Abnormally prominent anterior tibial tubercle – clinical and X-ray appearance. This is usually of no significance but may be vulnerable to knocks and kicks.

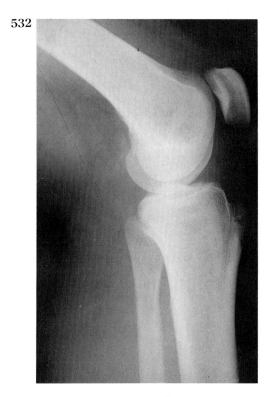

532 Fragmented tubercle with loose body – often a source of pain requiring removal.

15 Lower leg injuries

Lower limb injuries in sport are extremely common, as a result of both direct and indirect violence, and of overuse. Apart from basic fractures and soft-tissue injuries, a number of special conditions are met in sport which may cause problems.

Differential diagnosis is sometimes difficult unless the particular mechanism of the sport involved is borne in mind. It is important to note that a number of painful conditions in the lower limb may be associated with foot deformities. This is particularly true of the inflammatory lesions affecting the stirrup tendons and the muscles that power them.

Stress fractures

Management of stress fractures always involves reduction or cessation of stressful activity as well as symptomatic measures.

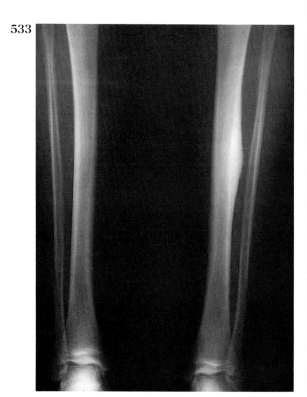

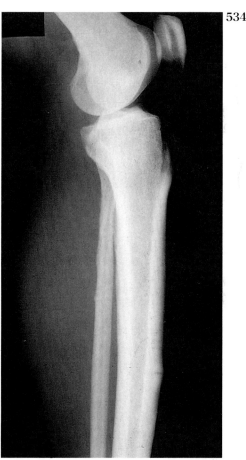

533 and **534** **Typical appearance of a stress fracture,** in the junction of the upper and middle thirds of the tibia in a 400-metre track athlete (**533**), and at the junction of the middle and lower thirds of the tibia in a jogger (**534**).

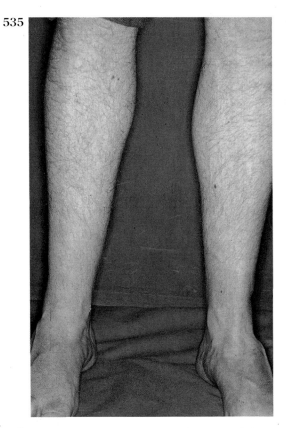

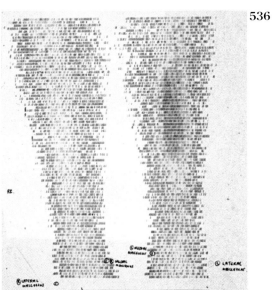

536 Technetium 99 bone scan showing a 'hot node' in the tibia.

535 Clinical appearance of a stress fracture of the tibia showing thickening of the bone.

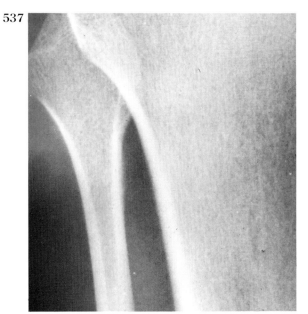

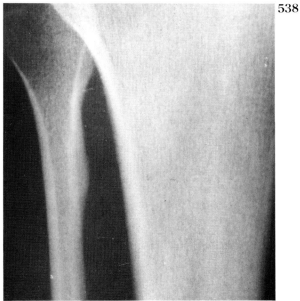

537 and 538 Development of fibula stress fracture: X-ray appearance three weeks after onset of symptoms (**537**) and seven months later (**538**).

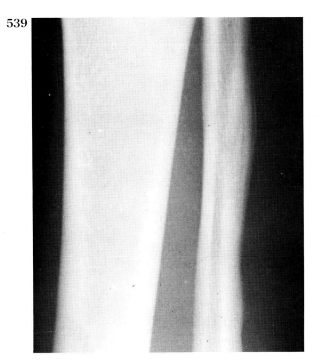

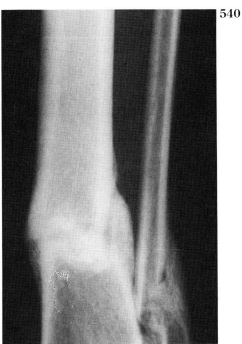

539 Fibula showing stress fracture at the junction of middle and lower thirds in a soccer player.

540 Tibia and fibula – a united old fracture with recent stress fracture visible in the fibula above the site of the original fracture. Stress fracture in the fibula is not uncommon in patients undergoing intensive rehabilitation for return to sport after major fractures of the lower limb.

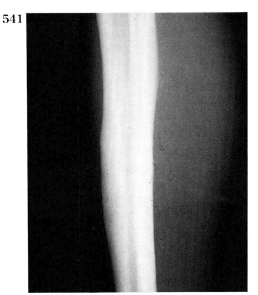

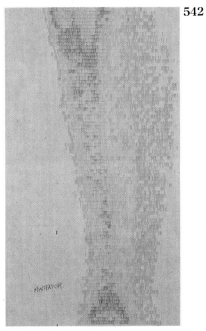

541 Anterior tibial cortical hyperplasia. This is the other stress response, usually painful and difficult to differentiate from stress fracture. Note the marked narrowing of the medullary canal (the patient is a marathon runner).

542 Cortical hyperplasia scan showing relatively uniform increase in uptake throughout the length of the tibia.

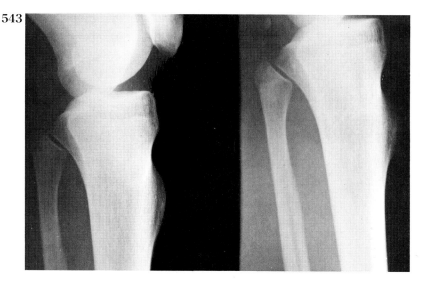

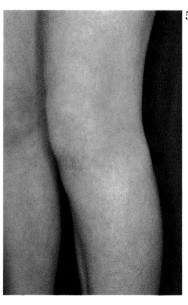

544

543 Benign exostisis (not Osgood-Schlatter's disease) – vulnerable to knocks playing soccer.

544 Superior tibiofibular joint subluxation. A cause of pain with excessive mobility of the clinically prominent fibular head.

Shin pain

Shin pain, otherwise known as 'shin splints' or 'shin soreness', is a portmanteau term referring to the symptoms of pain in the anterior aspect of the lower leg. The conditions involved are essentially due to overuse and may be acute, as in the case of anterior tibial compartment syndrome, but are more commonly chronic.

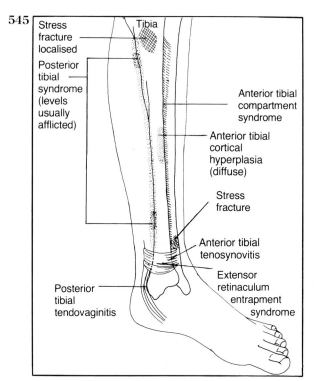

545 Differential diagnosis of shin pain.

Posterior tibial syndrome

Posterior tibial syndrome (sometimes known as medial tibial syndrome) is due to tearing away of the muscle fascia from the medial border of the tibia, with subsequent scar tissue formation.

546

546 Posterior tibial syndrome. This type of leg with the low soleus insertion is typical of the patient with posterior tibial syndrome.

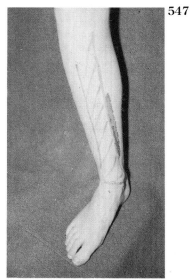

547

547 Posterior tibial syndrome – the site of pain and tenderness along the medial tibial border.

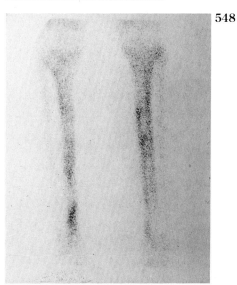

548

548 Radionucleide scan showing patchy 'hot nodes' in the tibia.

Decompression of the posterior tibial compartment relieves pain, permitting free movement of the muscles within. Similar types of procedure can be used for anterior tibial compartment syndrome.

549 Extensive open decompression for posterior tibial compartment syndrome. The patient has subsequently competed as a cross-country running international.

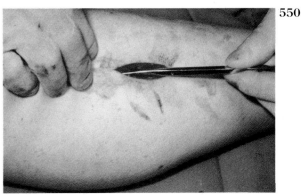

550 Closed decompression using a special fasciotome which leaves a smaller, neater scar.

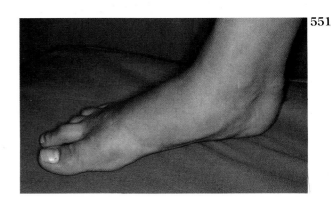

551 Pronating foot – collapse of the foot into pronation due to failure of the tibialis posterior to act effectively as a stirrup in posterior tibial syndrome.

Anterior tibial syndrome

This is more truly a compartment syndrome, as raised intramuscular pressure is the prime cause. In established cases decompression of the very thick strong anterior tibial fascia is required.

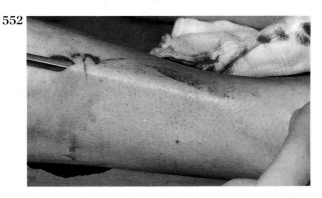

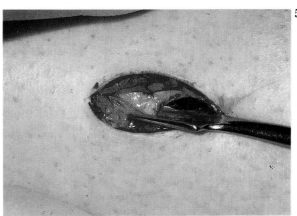

552 and **553 Anterior tibial decompression.** Note the thickness of the fascia (**553**).

Diverse problems

Other problems involving the lower leg from time to time cause a degree of diagnostic confusion. The most important thing to remember is that there is a wide variety of possibilities and that many cases of pain are associated with disorders of gait, often due to constitutional structural anomalies in the leg or foot.

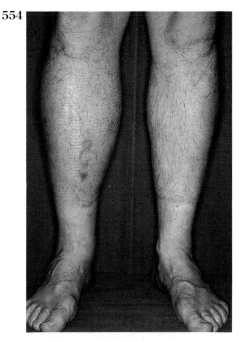

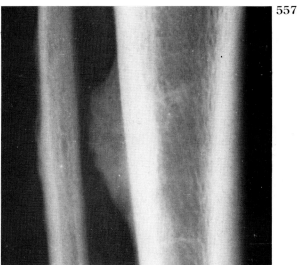

555 Ectopic calcification (cause unknown) in this middle-distance runner – possibly calcification in extravasated blood from old interstitial bleeding. The patient complained of persistent pain and inability to train.

554 Subperiosteal haematoma as a result of a direct blow on the front of the shin of a field hockey player.

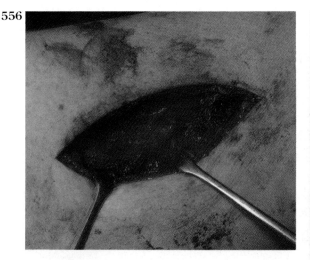

556 Cock's-comb tibia at operation, showing the removal of the 'cock's-comb' exostosis of the tibia, which is also associated with pain when running. The patient subsequently resumed his sport without further pain.

557 An X-ray of the lesion in 556.

558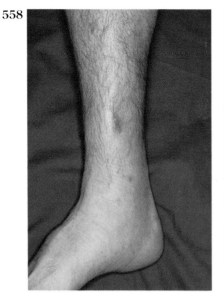

559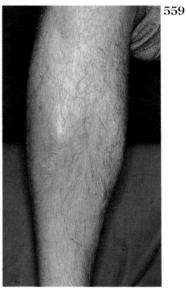

558 Localized haematoma. Small localized haematomas are very common over the shin and are often associated with the failure of absorption of the extravasated blood, leading to the development of cysts filled with dark 'black-currant jelly' clots. These haematomas dissolve very slowly if managed conservatively, so the treatment of choice is surgical evacuation.

559 Secondary cellulitis in a pretibial haematoma.

560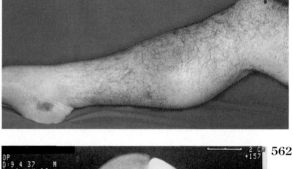

560 Muscle tear – partial rupture in the belly of the gastrocnemius.

561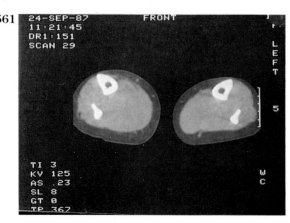

562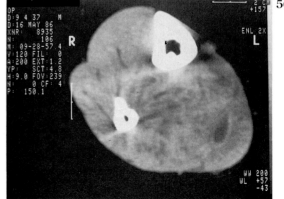

561 and **562 Gastrocnemius tears.** Compare the CT scan showing a diffuse lesion in the muscle belly (**561**) with a similar scan of an encysted lesion with clearly defined walls in a chronic case (**562**).

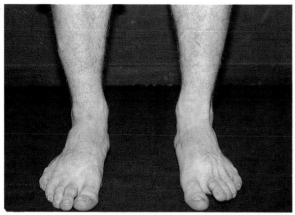

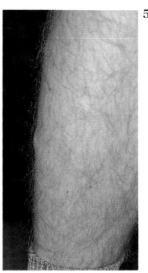

563 and **564 Venous blow out** – increased pressure in the deep venous channels during exercise may cause the perforating veins to blow out, producing varicosities.

Tibial torsion

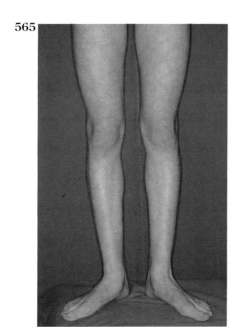

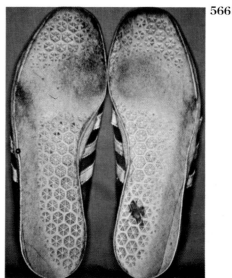

566 Uneven wear on the shoes of the patient featured in 565. Normal wear is from the outer side of the heel to the inner side of the sole.

565 Tibial torsion. An example of tibial torsion associated with valgus feet.

16 Achilles tendon injuries

Achilles tendon pain is a problem in sport. Complete rupture is usually intrinsic but the patient often complains that he has been struck on the back of the leg. The diagnosis should be clearcut except in the untreated chronic case, where bloodclot bridging the gap between the tendon ends may cast some doubts. The main problem is in differentiating between lesions of the tendon and those of the surrounding tissues (paratenon). Differentiation is usually relatively easy with the movement test. Many of the pathological changes in Achilles tendon pain can co-exist – for example, focal degeneration and chronic peritendonitis.

The movement test

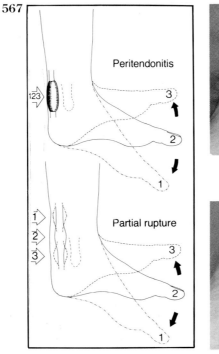

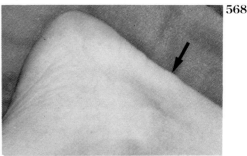

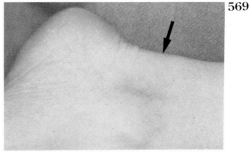

567 Differential diagnosis of tendon and paratenon lesions. Diagrammatic representation of the fixed position of the swelling and inflammation of peritendonitis as compared with the obvious movement of the lesion within the tendon with excursion of the foot.

568 and **569 A tendon lesion** with the foot in the neutral (**568**) and full plantar (**569**) flexion. Note the obvious movement of the point of swelling in the tendon in relation to the medial malleolus.

Complete rupture

Although conservative management has its protagonists, the optimum treatment for complete rupture in sportsmen is almost invariably surgical repair.

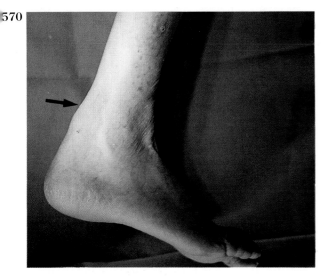

570 Ruptured tendon – note the obvious 'dent' in the tendon outline proximal to the stump of tendon (arrowed).

571 Tendon damage demonstrated at operation for surgical repair.

Partial rupture

Partial rupture is always of sudden onset. The treatment depends on the extent of the rupture and the disability it causes. In minor cases it may be managed as focal degeneration (see below), but a period of immobilization in plaster of Paris (with surgery in severe cases) is often required.

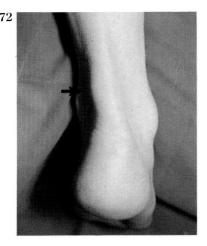

572 Clinical appearances are similar to tendonitis but will depend upon the extent of the damage.

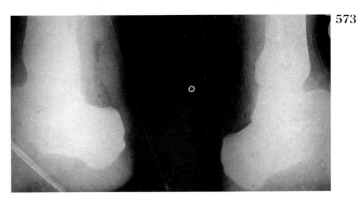

573 X-ray showing distortion of soft tissue shadow and some infiltration of Kager's triangle. The latter is a sign of reaction in the tissues surrounding the tendon.

Different types of partial rupture

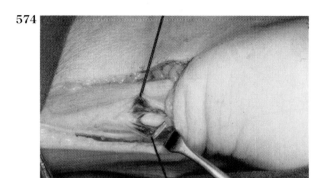

574 A minor partial rupture on the subcutaneous surface in a jogger.

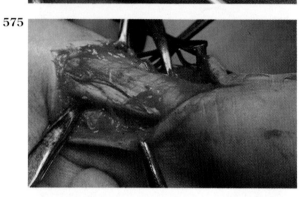

575 Partial rupture extending into the tendon but with no gross loss of continuity, in an international soccer player.

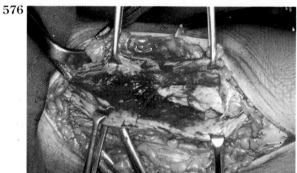

576 Gross partial rupture with loss of continuity of the gastrocnemius component, in a netball player.

Focal degeneration

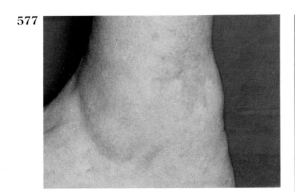

577 Focal degeneration – quite well-localized swelling on the tendon.

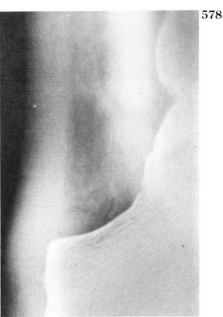

578 Focal degeneration – the soft-tissue shadow of the tendon shows a fusiform expansion.

579 Operative photograph showing a small area of degeneration with granulation tissue in the centre of the tendon, in a 400-metres runner.

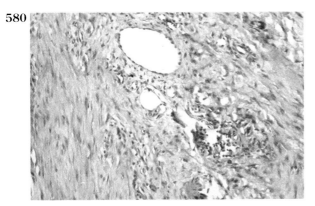

580 Histological appearance. Note the 'wet tissue paper' effect with lacunae in the tendon tissue and new blood vessel formation.

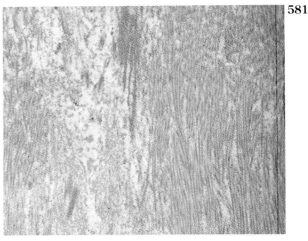

581 Electron microscopy showing organelles associated with tissue damage and darker threads of disordered elastin. Note the normal collagen banding. This appearance closely resembles that of tissues which have been exposed to excessive therapeutic insonation.

Symptoms of focal degeneration develop insidiously. The condition appears to be the result of repeated microtrauma (overuse injury) in a relatively avascular tissue which does not allow for adequate or effective healing. In established cases tenolysis is required.

Tendonitis

Onset of symptoms in tendonitis is also gradual. The tendon is more widely and diffusely tender and swollen, but will more readily respond to rest, a heel raise and physiotherapy.

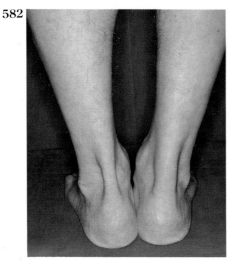

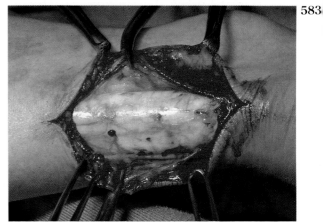

583 Fusiform thickening of tendon at operation.

582 Achilles tendonitis – typical diffuse swelling, palpable subcutaneously.

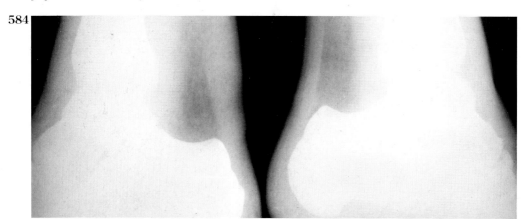

584 X-ray appearance showing thickening of soft tissue shadow of tendon but no infiltration of Kager's triangle.

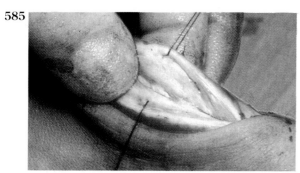

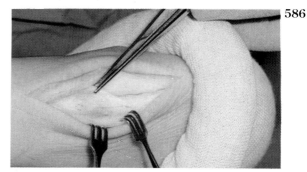

585 Appearance at operation without a tourniquet, showing loss of normal glistening appearance and bulging of cut surfaces due to local oedema (a jogger).

586 Operation under tourniquet, showing discoloration due to haemorrhage into the tendon (a soccer player).

Peritendonitis

Peritendonitis when acute (often with crepitus) usually responds well to multipoint injections of local anaesthetic and hyaluronidase. Steroids are seldom needed. When the condition is chronic and fibrotic, however, surgery becomes virtually the only means of securing return to full activity.

Note that in some cases the adherent chronically scarred paratenon may become so grossly thickened as not only to cause irritation due to friction between tendon and paratenon but mechanically to limit excursion of the tendon within the sheath. Excision of the paratenon does not appear significantly to prejudice the blood supply of the tendon in these cases.

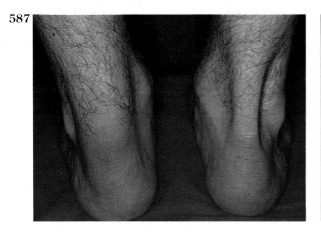

587 Diffuse thickening around the Achilles tendon typical of Achilles peritendonitis.

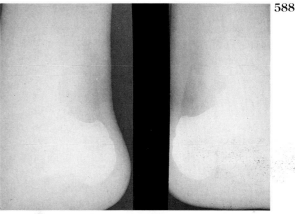

588 Soft tissue X-ray of the Achilles tendon showing obliteration of Kager's triangle.

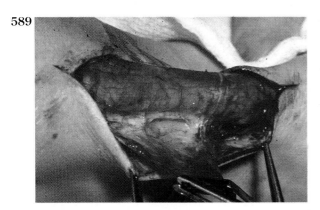

589 Dense adhesions around the Achilles tendon at operation, in a 1500-metres international runner.

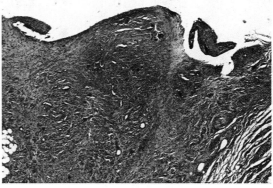

590 Histology of paratenon showing evidence of old and new scar tissue formation, deposits of fibrin and extravasated blood.

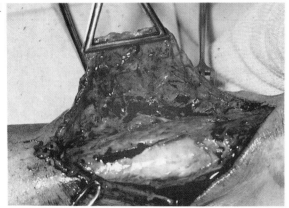

591

591 Failure to excise the paratenon in surgery for chronic Achilles tendon pain is the commonest cause of recurrence. Appearance at re-operation.

Mixed lesions

Inflammation of both tendon and paratenon frequently leads to a mixed lesion with features of all the pathologies present.

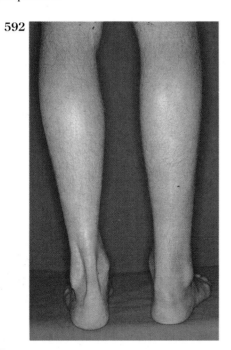

592

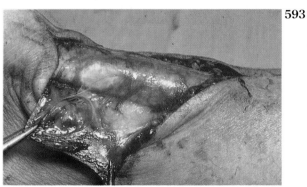

593

593 Mixed lesion at operation showing adherent paratenon and obviously abnormal tendon.

592 Clinical appearance of mixed lesion with diffuse swelling of the paratenon and secondary muscle wasting due to the tendon lesion.

Bursitis

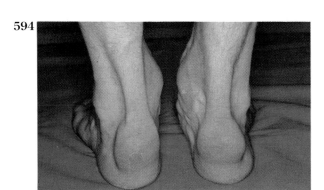

594 Typical clinical appearance of Achilles tendon bursitis, often associated with ill-fitting sports shoes.

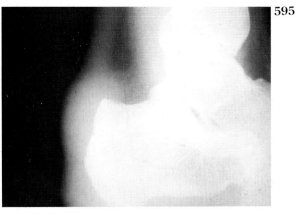

595 X-ray appearance of Achilles tendon bursitis, showing swelling marked by soft tissue shadow.

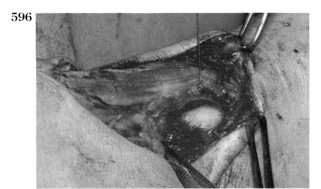

596 Operative appearance of bursa deep to the Achilles tendon, associated with a mass of granulation tissue within the bursa requiring curettage.

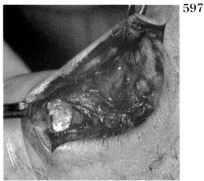

597 Operative appearance of bursa superficial to the tendon. The bursa has been packed with gauze to demonstrate its cavity more readily.

Calcified bursitis

Early cases will respond to shortwave diathermy. When chronic, surgical excision may be necessary. In all cases, attention must be paid to the need for suitable footwear.

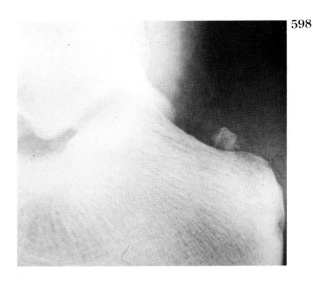

598 Calcification in deep Achilles tendon bursa demonstrated by X-ray.

Ectopic calcification

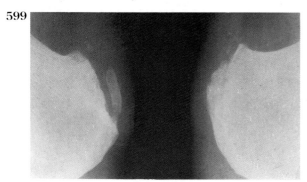

599 Ectopic calcification in the Achilles tendon at its insertion.

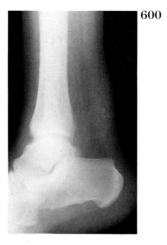

600 Ectopic calcification in the tendon itself. Actual bone may be laid down in some instances.

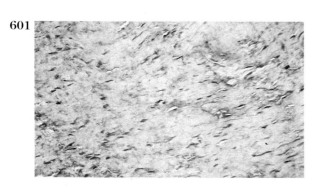

601 Ectopic chondrification – histology showing cartilage deposit in the degenerate Achilles tendon.

Insertion lesions

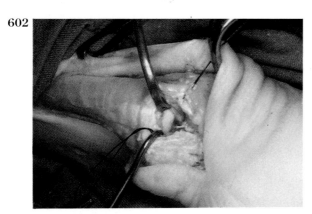

602 Insertion lesion – operative photograph showing nidus of granulation tissue in erosion of the Achilles tendon insertion. Probably a chronic traction injury.

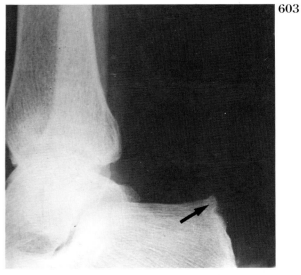

603 X-ray showing small erosion in the posterior aspect of the calcaneum associated with Achilles insertion lesion. Resistant cases may require surgical curettage.

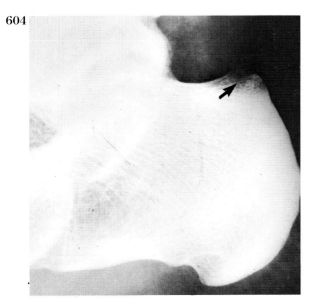

604 X-ray of the heel showing small exostosis at the Achilles tendon insertion, often associated with chronic deep Achilles tendon bursa.

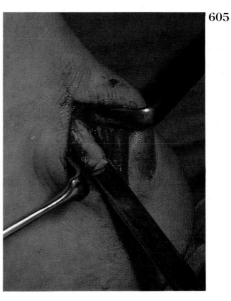

605 Excision of calcaneal exostosis at operation.

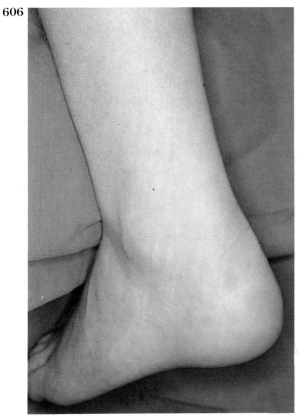

606 Avulsion of calcaneal apophysis – clinical appearance.

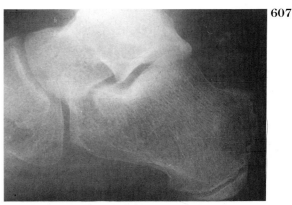

607 Avulsion of insertion on calcaneal apophysis in a young soccer player – X-ray appearance.

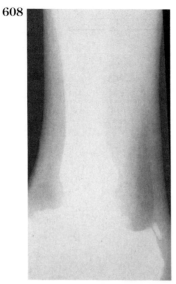

608 Avulsion of Achilles tendon attachment in an adult – X-ray appearance.

Musculotendonous junction

Partial tears of the musculotendonous junction (as indeed tears in the gastrocnemius more proximally) are often misdiagnosed as 'ruptured plantaris tendon'. The latter condition has not in fact been shown to exist. Treatment of musculotendonous junction injury is in accordance with the usual management of muscle or tendon injury, depending on the component structure most affected.

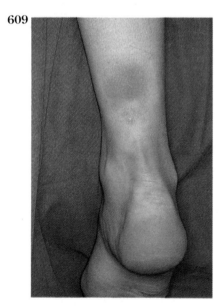

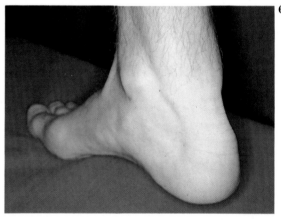

610 Musculotendonous junction – congenital abnormality. In this case presenting with peritendonitis the soleus was inserted directly with no tendon onto the superior aspect of the calcaneum.

609 Clinical appearance in a long jumper of musculotendonous junction lesion showing bruising of overlying skin. This lesion is an acute instantaneous intrinsic injury very similar to a muscle tear and the result of uncoordinated explosive effort.

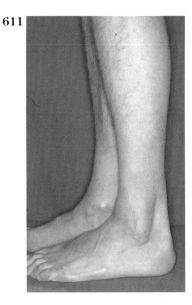

611 Musculotendonous junction tear showing defect at the site of lesion.

Complications of steroid therapy

Treatment of tendon lesions by steroid injection is contraindicated in view of the strong risk of subsequent tendon rupture. This is particularly exemplified in the Achilles tendon. Even the treatment of peritendonitis by injection may leave chronic deposits in the tissue.

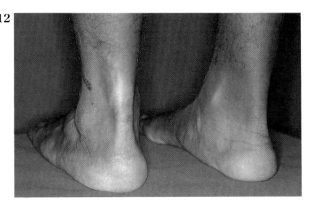

612 Steroid stigmata – depigmentation and loss of subcutaneous fat after steroid injection.

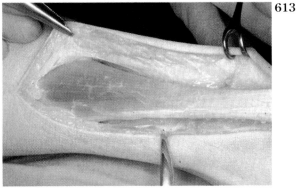

613 Chalky deposits in the paratenon associated with the injection of depot steroid preparations: the tendon itself is intact. Pallor is caused by application of tourniquet.

614 Partial rupture of the Achilles tendon due to injection of steroid directly into the tendon.

615 Complete rupture of the Achilles tendon due to injection of steroid directly into the tendon.

Complications of surgery

Achilles tendon surgery has become more popular in efforts to restore function to sportsmen suffering from chronic Achilles tendon pain. It is not without its problems, however, most of which relate to the skin wound – this area is notorious for poor healing.

Wound dehiscence may occur with too energetic mobilization in the early stages, particularly if the patient tries to do too much on his own. The chronic problem is hypertrophic scar tissue formation.

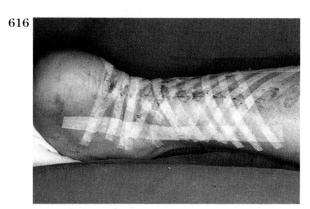

616 Immediately post-operative, showing the wound closed with Steristrips. (Latter are used to distribute the strain over the surrounding skin and to avoid the use of sutures, which are liable to cause wound necrosis.)

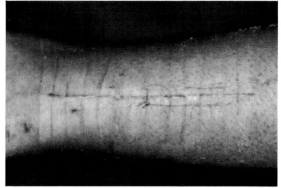

617 After removal of Steristrips on the 12th post-operative day.

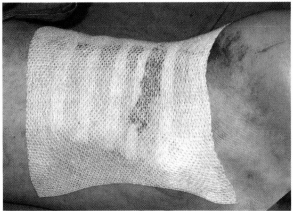

618 Localized wound margin overload may occur with small areas of breakdown even with Steristrips. Use of an elastic adhesive net dressing such as Mefix distributes the load more evenly and gives better protection from wound breakdown.

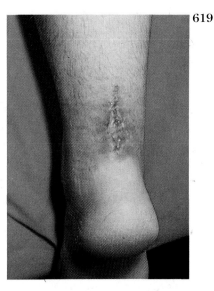

619 Early post-operative complication – wound dehiscence (typically at the lower end) is often associated with uncontrolled and excessive activity during the early post-operative (2–3 weeks) rehabilitation phase. Overtight sutures may produce marginal necrosis in the wound at an earlier stage.

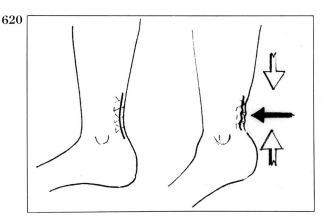

620 Early wound breakdown mechanism – gastrocnemius spasm causing forced plantar flexion, a potent cause of early wound breakdown.

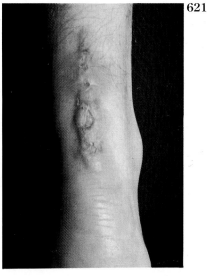

621 Late complication – hypertrophic scar tissue formation with cracking. This may be treated by injection of steroid directly into the scar or alternatively by wearing an elastic (eg, Jobst) support.

17 Ankle injuries

Congenital abnormalities

Congenital abnormalities cause problems by their mechanical interference with the full range of joint movement.

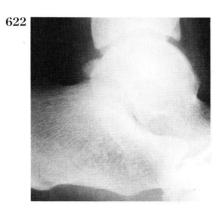

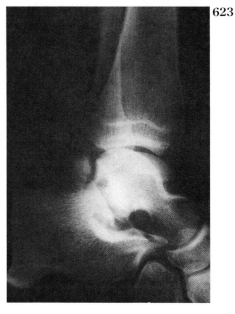

622 Prominent talar spur – X-ray appearance (see **625**).

623 Os trigonum X-ray. Note the small impingement exostosis on the anterior margin of the tibia. This was causing pain and impaired performance in an international decathlete.

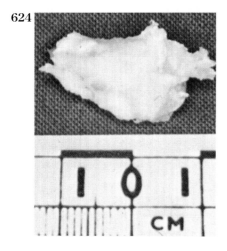

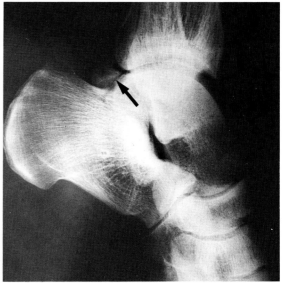

624 Os trigonum specimen after removal. The joint between the os trigonum and the talus may show evidence of chondromalacia.

625 Mechanics of interference. The os trigonum (or posterior talar spur) becomes the nut in the nutcracker of the tibia and calcaneum in forced flexion.

626 Impingement exostosis on the calcaneum (note also similar exostosis on the talus).

Osteochondritis

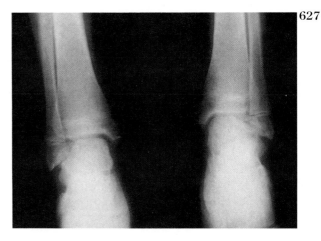

627 Osteochondritis of the talus associated with congenital abnormality causing pain and swelling in a teenage soccer player.

Ankle injury

Ankle injury is common in sport and is often associated with unsuitable footwear. It is seen particularly in soccer and skiing, and ranges in severity from fracture dislocation to simple ligament sprain.

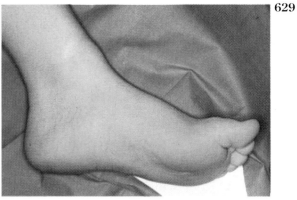

628 Skiing accidents are a potent cause of major ankle injuries, particularly if the boots rather than the bindings give way.

629 Fracture dislocation of the ankle joint – clinical appearance.

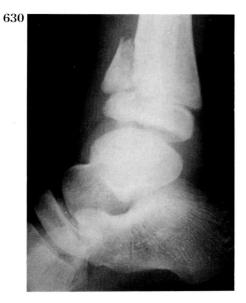

630 Fracture of the ankle with dislocation of the inferior tibial epiphysis.

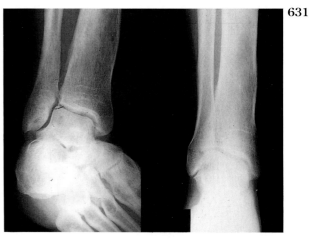

631 Old ankle fracture with epiphyseal damage in a young soccer player.

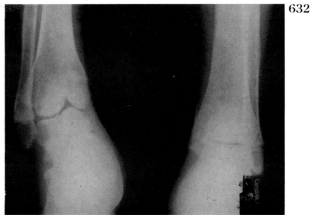

632 Deformity due to distortion of bone growth. As with epiphyseal damage at the elbow, close follow-up monitoring is necessary.

Sprains

The 'typical' sprain of the ankle involves the lateral collateral ligament as a result of an inversion injury. Other sprains are relatively unusual.

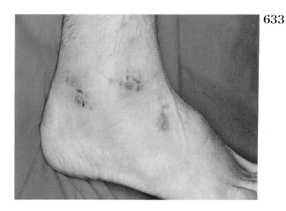

633 Simple sprain of the lateral ligament – clinical appearance. This is the commonest ankle injury.

Types of sprain

Some ankle sprains appear very severe when there is gross swelling and ecchymosis, although these are often cases in which the least significant damage is done. The possibility of associated bone injury must always be borne in mind, however. Demonstration of clinical instability may require examination under a general anaesthetic with stress X-rays or screening.

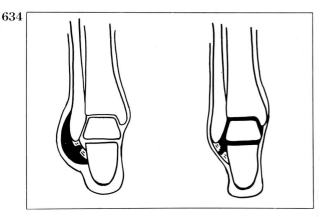

634 'Internal' and 'external' sprains. Internal sprains are associated with haemarthrosis, without gross external swelling. External sprains are associated with marked swelling and external bruising.

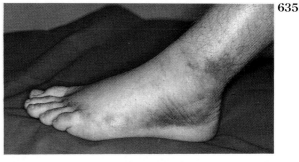

635 An 'external' type of lateral collateral ligament sprain showing dramatic appearance.

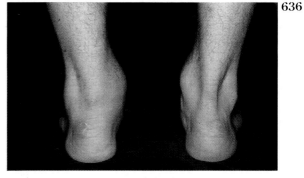

636 'Internal' type of ankle sprain. Swelling is only really noticeable behind the ankle joint due to bulging of the posterior capsule under the pressure of the haemarthrosis, which produces swelling on both sides of the Achilles tendon.

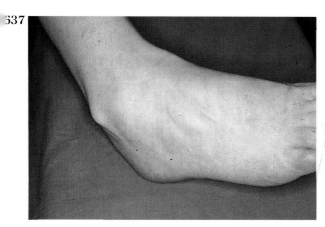

637 Clinical signs of instability in collateral ligament rupture – the lateral malleolus becomes more prominent as the talus tilts on inversion.

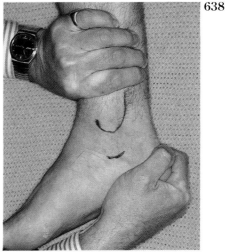

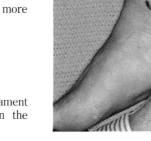

638 Eliciting the anterior drawer sign – in ligament rupture the talus may be displaced forwards in the mortice.

Radiological appearance in ligament rupture

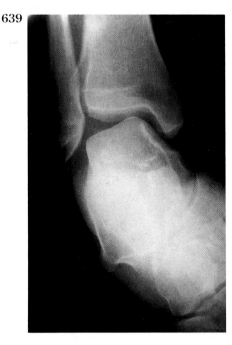

639

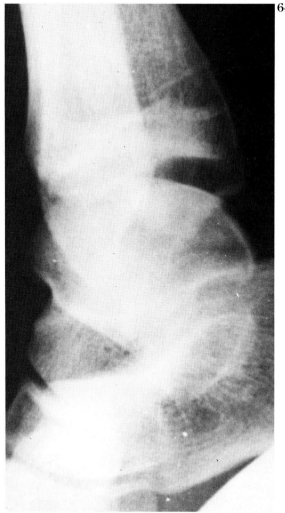

639 and **640** **Severe cases of damage to supporting ligaments** will cause the ligament to give way and the joint to become unstable. These stress X-rays show talar tilt in tear of the lateral collateral ligament and subluxation of the talus (forward tilt) in posterior capsular tear – a forced dorsiflexion injury in a young gymnast.

Note that the ankle is commonly a site of 'stable instability'.

641

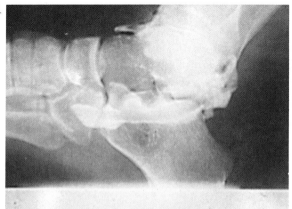

641 Communication between peroneal tendon sheaths and ankle joint is only present as a normal finding in a small proportion of subjects. Demonstration of such a connection by arthrogram may therefore support a diagnosis of ligament rupture which causes a pathological communication.

Impingement exostosis – 'footballer's ankle'

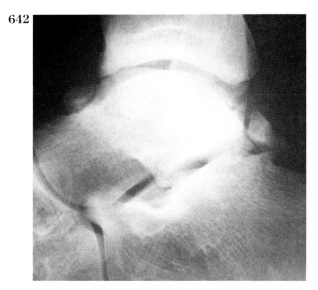

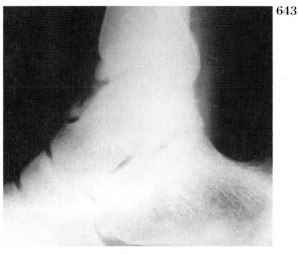

642 Footballer's ankle. Impingement exostoses and marginal osteophyte formation. Note that the joint gap is normal; this is not degenerative joint disease and the articular cartilage is not thinned. There is also an os trigonum present which in this case may be an old fractured talar spur.

643 Example of solitary impingement exostosis on the neck of the talus with osteophytes also showing on the anterior aspect of the lower tibia.

Degenerative joint disease

Clinically the joint may appear normal or there may be visible and palpable thickening. Crepitus is sometimes marked and there may be obvious limitation of movement.

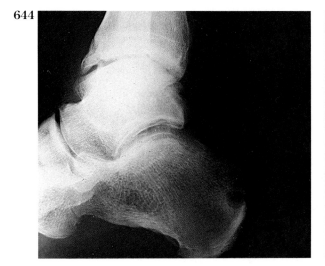

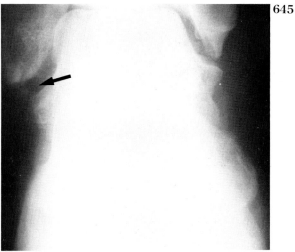

644 Osteoarthrosis. Typical X-ray appearance of degenerative joint disease of the ankle joint with narrowing of the joint space and marginal osteophyte formation.

645 'Joint mice'. Minute loose body in the ankle joint of a young middle-distance runner.

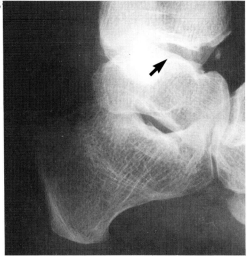

646 Osteochondritis dissecans showing distortion of the talus.

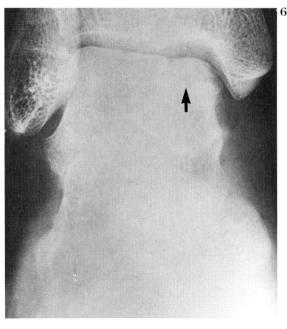

647 Anteroposterior X-ray showing fragment separate from talus.

Osteochondritis dissecans is an uncommon cause of loose-body formation in the ankle joint – the most common is post-traumatic osteoarthrosis. Loose bodies in the ankle joint may cause considerable disability by jamming in the mortice; even very small loose bodies can cause severe symptoms. Treatment is surgical removal.

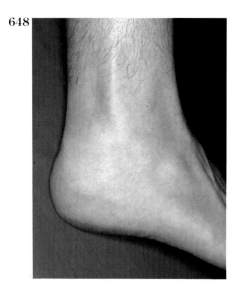

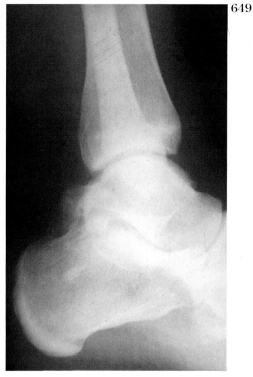

648 and **649 This patient complained of the gradual onset of swelling and discomfort behind the right ankle.** He was thought to have a chronic peroneal tendovaginitis. The X-ray showed a marked talar spur and also traces of calcification posterior to the tibia. At exploration this was found to be a benign ossifying chondroma.

Heel

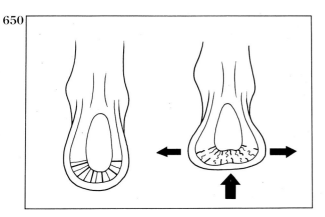

650 Heel-bruising mechanism. Note that a stress fracture of the calcaneum is occasionally demonstrable.

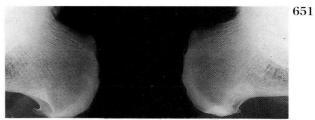

651 Calcaneal spur – X-ray appearance.

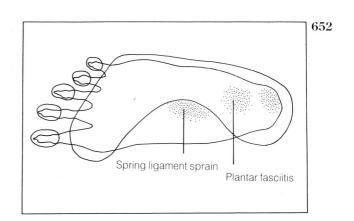

Spring ligament sprain

Plantar fasciitis

652 Plantar fasciitis – clinical features and differential diagnosis.

Both calcaneal spur and plantar fasciitis respond to the provision of a high-arch valgus insole with substantial heel padding, ultrasonics, or anti-inflammatory medication topical or systemic. Chronic cases require surgery.

Tendon lesions

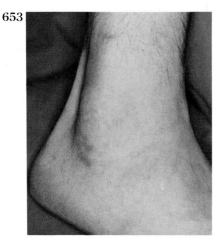

653 Snapping or subluxing peroneal tendons.

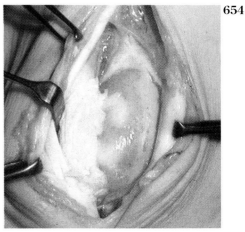

654 Subluxing peroneal tendon – appearance at operation showing degenerated tendon and grossly widened tendon sheath.

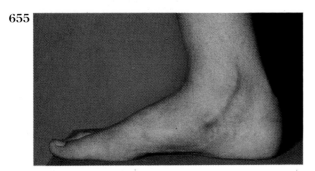

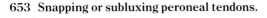

655 Posterior tibial tendovaginitis showing well-marked tendon with thickened sheath.

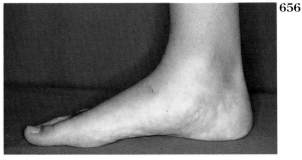

656 Tibialis posterior tendovaginitis – more usual appearance with diffuse swelling behind and below medial malleolus.

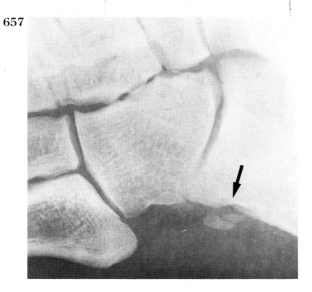

657 Calcification in tendon shown in the tendon of peroneus brevis, just proximal to insertion.

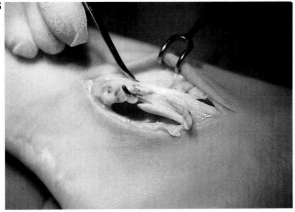

658 Peroneal tendon – partial rupture as seen at operation.

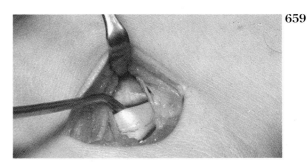

659 Tendovaginitis of extensor hallucis longus at operation, showing thickened tendon sheath.

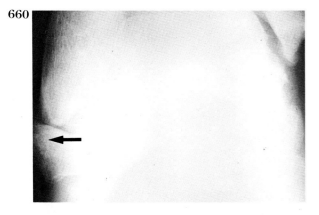

660 Peroneus brevis calcification. Not an accessory ossicle, but calcification in the tendon of peroneus brevis.

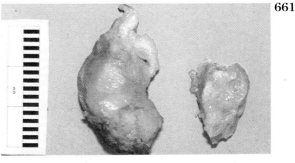

661 Operation specimen from 660.

Overuse injuries of the stirrup muscle tendons and their sheaths are common about the ankle and are frequently associated with functional deformity of the foot, particularly the collapse of the medial arch. Treatment, whether conservative or surgical, will often involve the provision of an orthosis to hold the foot in a neutral position and support the collapsing ray while the muscle regains its tone.

Extensor retinaculum entrapment syndrome

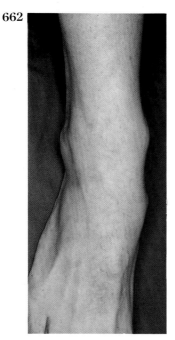

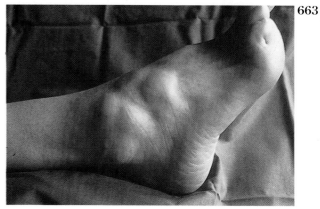

663 Well-marked chronic entrapment with marked secondary synovial effusion clearly outlining the extensor retinaculum.

662 Extensor retinaculum entrapment syndrome showing swelling over dorsum of ankle.

664 Extensor retinaculum demonstrated at operation.

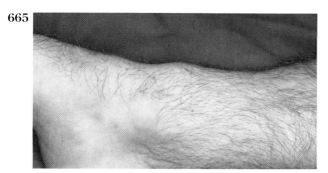

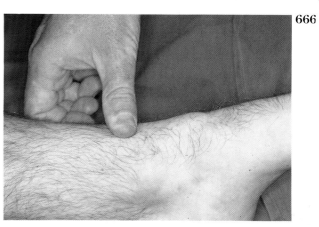

665 and **666 Small effusion associated with entrapment** which can be balloted above and below the retinaculum.

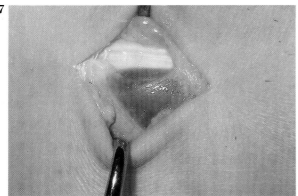

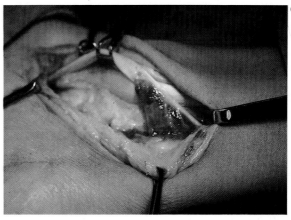

667 Extensor retinaculum entrapment syndrome.
Operation for decompression showing muscle fibres inserting into the tendon distal to the retinaculum.

668 Pigmented villo-nodular synovitis at operation — an unusual cause of tendon pain.

18 Foot injuries

Abnormalities

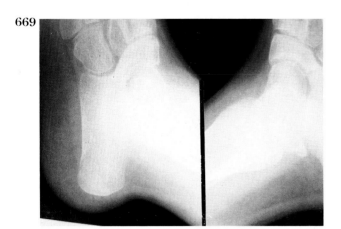

669 X-ray of the foot showing a calcaneonavicular bar – a cause of spastic flat foot.

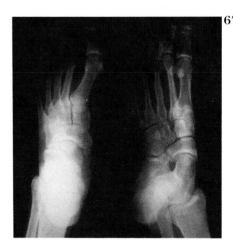

670 Abnormal calcaneonavicular articulations – a cause of painful flat foot in a runner.

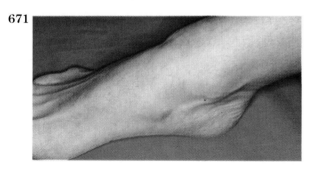

671 Clinical appearance of the navicular ossicle showing prominence over the navicular on the medial side of the foot. This causes pain due to arthrosis in articulation with the main bone.

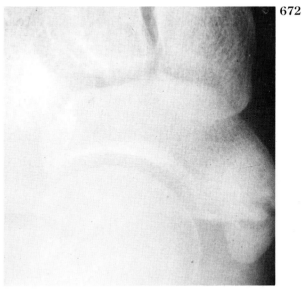

672 X-ray showing os naviculare – an accessory ossicle on the navicular.

Tarsal abnormalities are occasionally met and may be a cause of so-called 'spastic flat foot'. As a rule, simple supportive measures are all that is needed – but where the abnormality is biomechanically significant, surgical intervention may be required or the patient may even have to give up vigorous sporting activity.

Tarsal fractures/dislocations

Tarsal injuries should be treated by rest and support in the early stages, and, after the pain has subsided, by appropriate mobilization including attention to intrinsic muscle build-up.

673
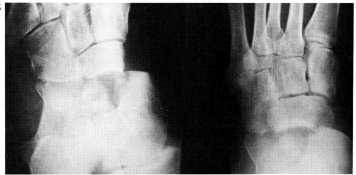

673 X-ray showing midtarsal dislocation in a patient after an accident motorcycle scrambling.

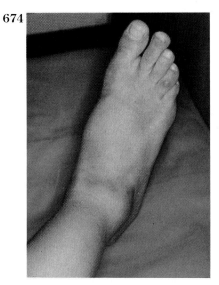

674 Gymnast's foot after subluxation of medial ray in a bad landing from a vault.

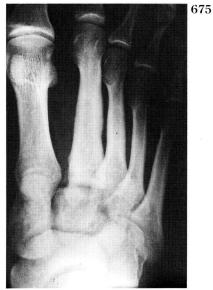

675 X-ray appearance of 674.

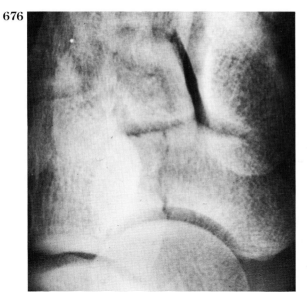

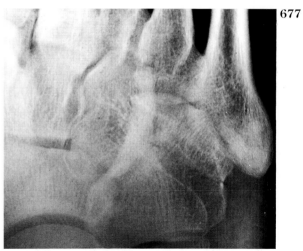

677 Fracture of cuboid – an unusual soccer injury.

676 Stress fracture of navicular in a young track athlete – a cause for foot pain often misdiagnosed and as often not recognized.

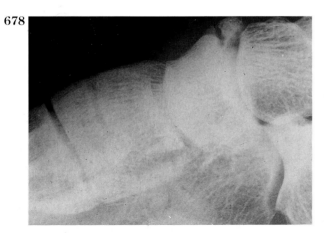

678 Impingement rim fracture of the navicular.

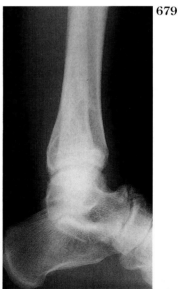

679 Osteoarthrosis (post-traumatic) of the talo-navicular joint.

Flatfoot

Postural abnormalities of the foot should not be treated for their own sake, but only if they are associated with significant symptom production (whether in the foot or higher in the leg).

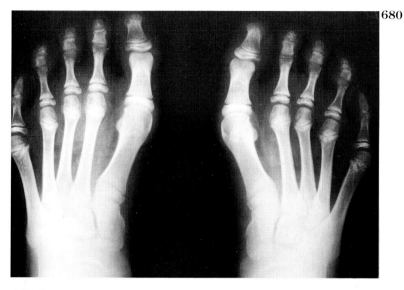

680

680 X-ray of broad foot showing metatarsus primus varus. When this condition is well marked a corrective osteotomy may be necessary. Patients with feet as broad as this need specially fitting shoes.

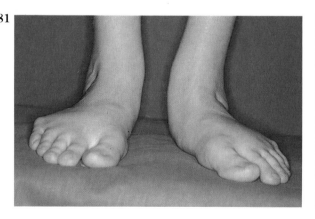

681

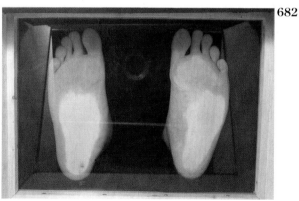

682

681 Valgus ankles associated with flatfoot – note the inward lean of the posterior calcaneum.

682 Load distribution in 'pes pancake' as shown on a mirror pedobarograph.

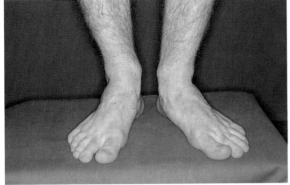

683 Flatfoot in a patient with torsion of the tibia. The flat appearance of the foot is of no clinical significance if function is good and the subject symptom-free.

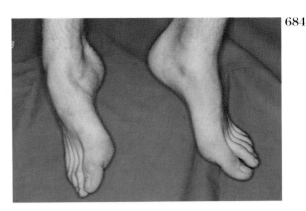

684 Spastic foot. A spastic foot held in inversion in a young athlete – a psychosomatic disturbance.

Osteochondritis

Osteochondritis is a relatively common cause of localized pain in the foot in sportsmen.

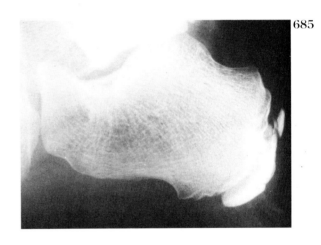

685 Sever's disease – osteochondritis of the calcaneal apophysis. Note that the X-ray appearances are very variable – this is really a clinical diagnosis. It appears to be an overuse traction lesion in adolescents.

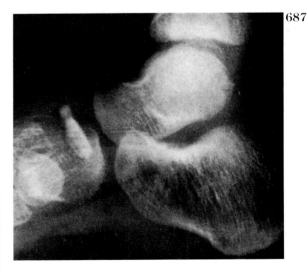

686 and 687 Kohler's disease – osteochondritis of the tarsal navicular leading to distortion of the bone.

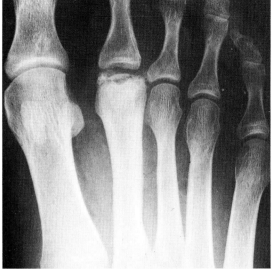

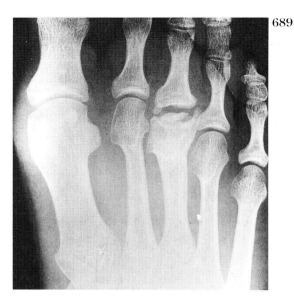

688 and **689 Freiburg's disease of the metatarsal heads.** Symptoms are due to arthrosis associated with incongruity of distorted joint surfaces.

Osteochondritis in the bones of the foot should be treated by rest. In Kohler's disease, in particular, distortion and subsequent osteoarthrosis frequently follow overenergetic mobilization while the disease is active.

Fractures of metatarsals, etc.

Metatarsal injuries are quite common in sport and are often of the overuse type. Chronic forefoot strain or metatarsalgia with no evidence of bone injury is often the result of exercise in unsuitable footwear on terrain to which the sportsman is not accustomed. Clinical features are pain but there are no obvious physical signs.

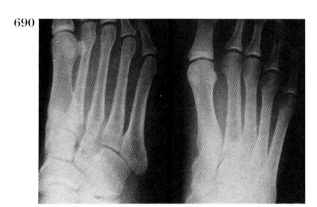

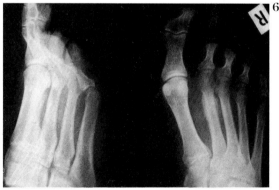

690 In early cases of stress fracture radiological change may be minimal (see **693**). This patient, a gymnast, presented with a three-week history of pain.

691 Stress fracture of the 2nd metatarsal.

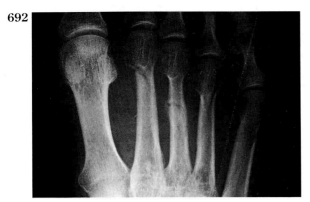

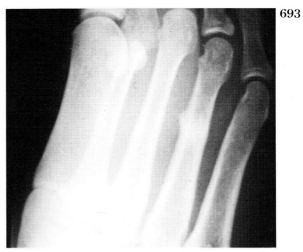

692 Stress fracture of the 3rd metatarsal.

693 Stress fracture of the 4th metatarsal. This X-ray was taken three weeks after 690.

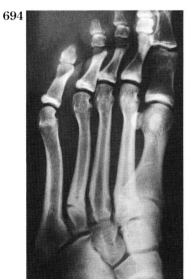

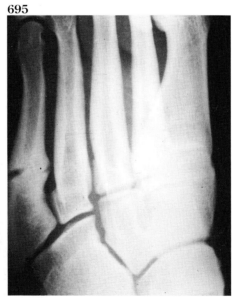

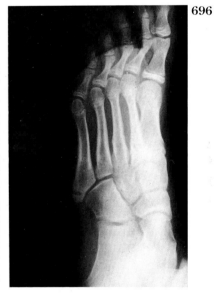

694 Fracture at the proximal end of the 4th metatarsal – cause uncertain. Compare with Jones' fracture.

695 Jones' fracture 5th metatarsal styloid. Another stress injury.

696 Fracture 5th metatarsal styloid due to avulsion stress.

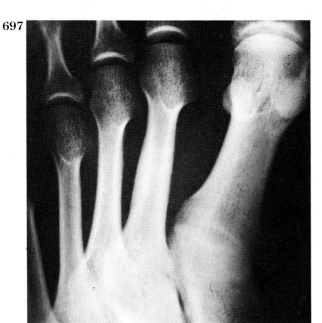

697

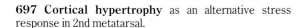

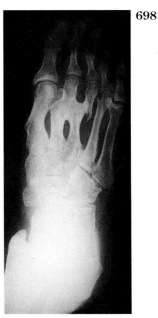

698

697 Cortical hypertrophy as an alternative stress response in 2nd metatarsal.

698 Old metatarsal fractures with malunion – presenting as a rigid, painful, flat foot in a jogger.

Morton's foot

In many patients the first metatarsal is shorter than the second (Morton's foot). It is argued that this particular arrangement with a long second toe makes the subject more prone to stress fractures of the metatarsals and to sesamoiditis, but this has not been confirmed in controlled studies. However, Morton's foot does make the management of hallux rigidus more difficult.

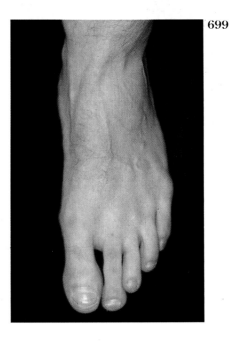

699

699 Morton's foot showing long second toe.

Metatarsalgia: other causes

Morton's metatarsalgia is an important cause of pain due to a neuroma developing on the interdigital nerve associated with rubbing between the metatarsal heads.

Treatment of metatarsalgia is essentially the treatment of cause. In functional metatarsalgia associated with overuse, contrast baths, supporting insoles (orthoses) or intrinsic muscle build-up is the treatment of choice.

700

Sensation: may be diminished in toe cleft

M-T head   M-T head   M-T head

Pain: on pressure from below
on movement of M-T heads
Diagrammatic cross-section between metatarsal heads to show clinical features of interdigital neuroma Morton's metatarsalgia .

700 Interdigital neuroma – clinical features.

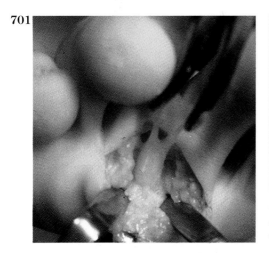

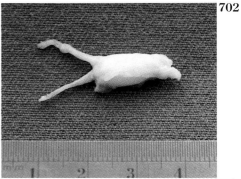

701 and **702 Interdigital neuroma,** at operation and (**702**) an operative specimen. Note the fusiform swelling on nerve and peripheral branches to contiguous toes.

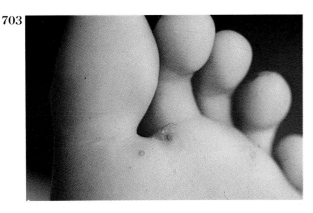

703 Verruca vulgaris – a condition which is often overlooked but is a very important cause of forefoot pain. It is due to a virus infection and may be highly contagious.

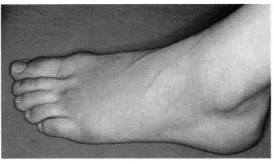

704 Extensor tenosynovitis on dorsum of foot (often due to bad lacing of shoes). To avoid unsatisfactory distribution of pressure, shoes with a long throat (ie, with more than 3 lace holes) should be laced with 2 laces, the proximal laces being tied tightly, the distal laces being tied loosely.

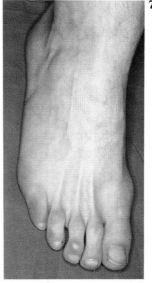

705 5th metatarsal bunion. Note the overlying callosity and those on toes 3–5, due to ill-fitting shoes on a foot abnormally broad even for an athlete.

Blisters

Blisters are often caused by ill-fitting shoes. They are readily treated by removing the dead skin and applying adhesive plaster directly over the raw area. It sounds drastic but is effective and remarkably comfortable for the patient.

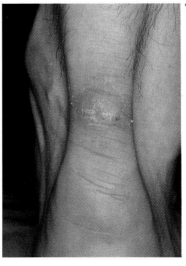

706 Blister. Too stiff a heel counter and tab rub on the tendo Achilles.

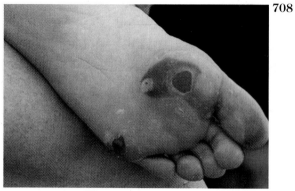

707 Blister. A broad foot needs a wide-fitting shoe. Sports footwear should be manufactured in a variety of fittings.

708 Blister. A stud or spike pushing through from below rubs under the forefoot.

Some oddities

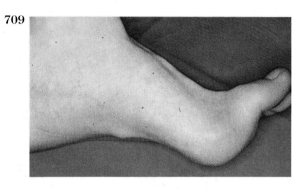

709 Inclusion dermoid in the sole of the foot.

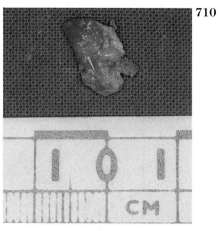

710 Fragment of artificial turf removed with inclusion dermoid from the foot.

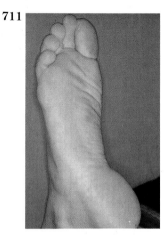

711 Plantar haematoma of unknown cause (spring ligament tear?) showing fullness on plantar aspect of the foot.

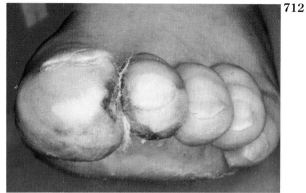

712 Cold injury – frostbite due to inadequate ski boots. A rather unusual example of the consequences of unsatisfactory footwear.

The toes

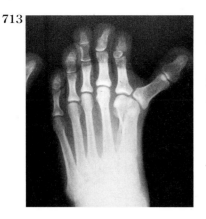

713 Congenital abnormality (major). Supernumerary toe in a young international soccer player required to wear boots. No problem after amputation.

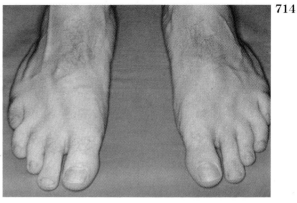

714 Congenital abnormality (minor). Note the alignment of the 4th and little toes. This shape of foot is of academic rather than clinical significance but may produce problems in shoe fitting.

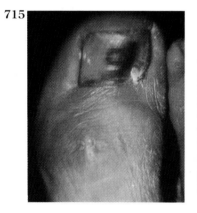

715 Subungual haematoma due to direct violence. A similar condition, resulting from ill-fitting shoes, is often seen affecting the toenails of the 1st and 2nd toes in long-distance runners.

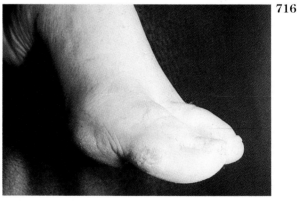

716 Callosity on the medial aspect of the toe and under the 1st metatarsophalangeal joint, the result of ill-fitting shoes in a long-distance runner.

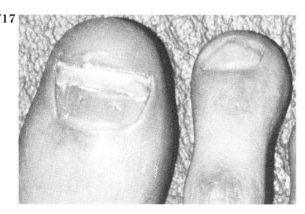

717 Nailbed damage to great toenail due to ill-fitting shoes.

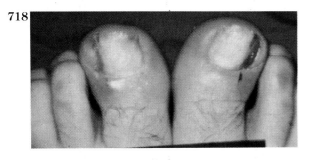

718 Ingrowing toenails – a common clinical problem in sportsmen.

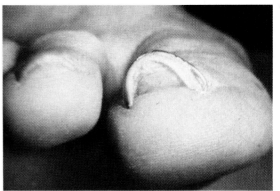

719 Subungual exostosis – clinical appearance.

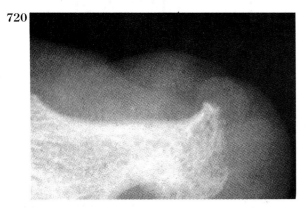

720 Subungual exostosis – X-ray appearance. The cause is uncertain, the treatment surgical, radical – and usually very effective.

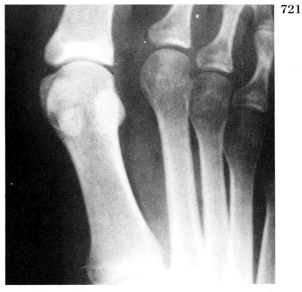

721 Sesamoiditis – anteroposterior X-ray showing disruption of the medial sesamoid under the first metatarsal head.

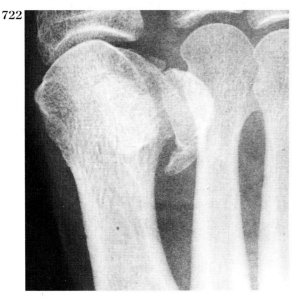

722 Sesamoiditis – old appearances with marginal osteophyte formation, in an oblique X-ray. Sesamoiditis is often due to inadequate padding or protection in the sole of the shoe or boot.

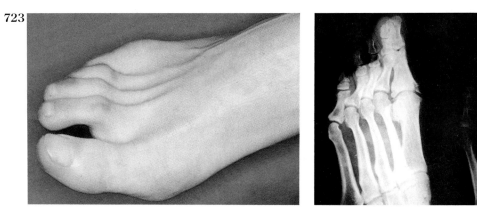

723 and **724** **Hallux rigidus in a middle-distance runner.** Clinical and radiological appearances. This condition may be extremely difficult to treat and the sufferer often has to abandon his athletic career prematurely.

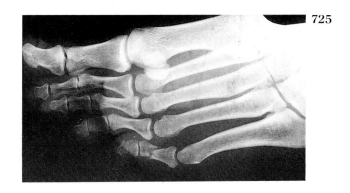

725 Fracture of proximal phalanx of 5th (little) toe from a kick – such fractures are disabling occasionally, but are nevertheless often neglected by the patient.

Further reading

Journals

American Journal of Sports Medicine
Published by: American Orthopedic Society for Sports Medicine, P.O. Box 9517, Columbus, GA 31908, USA.

British Journal of Sports Medicine
Published by: Butterworth Scientific Ltd, P.O. Box 63, Westbury House, Bury Street, Guildford, Surrey GU2 5BH, UK.
Subscriptions to: Westbury Subscription Services, P.O. Box 101, Sevenoaks, Kent TN15 8P1, UK.

International Journal of Sports Medicine
Published by: Georg Thieme Verlag, Rudigerstrasse 14, D-7000 Stuttgart 30, West Germany.

Journal of Sports Medicine and Physical Fitness
Published by: Edizioni Minerva Medica, Corso Bramante 83-85, 10126 Torino, Italy.

Medicine & Science in Sports & Exercise
Published by: American College of Sports Medicine, 401 West Michegan Street, Indianapolis, IN 46202, USA.

Physician & Sportsmedicine
Published by: McGraw Hill Inc., 4530 W 77th Street, Minneapolis, MN 55435, USA.

Sports Medicine
Published by: ADIS Press Ltd., 41 Centorian Drive, Mairangi Bay, Auckland 10, New Zealand.

Serial publications

Clinics in Sports Medicine
W.B. Saunders Co., Philadelphia, USA.

Medicine and Sport Science
Karger, Basel, Switzerland.

Year Book of Sports Medicine
Year Book Medical Publishers, Inc., Chicago, USA.

Books

Dirix, A., Knuttgen, H.G. & Tittel, K. (Eds)
The Olympic Book of Sports Medicine
(*Encyclopedia of Sports Medicine,* Volume 1)
Blackwell Scientific Publications, Oxford, 1988.

Helal, B., King, J. & Grange, W. (Eds)
Sports Injuries & Their Treatment
Chapman & Hall Medical, London, 1986.

O'Donoghue, D.
Treatment of Injuries to Athletes
Saunders, Philadelphia, 1983 (4th Ed).

Schneider, R.C., Kennedy, J.C. & Plant, M.L. (Eds)
Sports Injuries: Mechanisms, Prevention & Treatment
Williams & Wilkins, Baltimore, 1985.

Sperryn, P.N.
Sport and Medicine
Butterworths, London, 1983.

Williams, J.G.P. & Sperryn, P.N. (Eds)
Sports Medicine
Edward Arnold, London, 1976 (2nd Ed).

Index

All references are to page numbers